THE DAMASK CHEEK

The Damask Cheek

A COMEDY IN THREE ACTS

BY JOHN VAN DRUTEN

AND LLOYD MORRIS

RANDOM HOUSE · NEW YORK

Published simultaneously in Canada by
The Macmillan Company of Canada Limited

MANUFACTURED IN THE UNITED STATES OF AMERICA

To

FLORA

with our love

INTRODUCTION

By JOHN VAN DRUTEN

In presenting the printed version of *The Damask Cheek* to a reading public, it has occurred to me that people who are interested enough to buy a play may perhaps also be interested to know something of how it came to be written. Normally, the genesis of a play— the stages by which it passed from the first embryonic idea to the finished product played in the theatre—is something lost and forgotten, even by the author. Almost all of it having happened in his head and without record, he finds it impossible later to remember just how its component parts were arrived at or assembled. In the case of *The Damask Cheek,* for example, I myself had completely forgotten how I hit upon the title, until I was reminded by a chance remark after the opening night. I had assumed that it came directly from *Twelfth Night,* and that I must have either read or remembered the passage at some time during the writing of the play, taking the title straight from Shakespeare. At a party after the New York opening, however, I was introduced to a lady who asked me whether I knew that Haydn had set that passage to music, and I remembered suddenly that in January of this year I had gone to a recital by Lotte Lehmann, at which I had heard her sing that song, with a depth of feeling and a beauty of phrasing which brought the magic of the words to me with a poignancy that no reading or performance by an actress had ever given them before. The play itself was then exactly eleven pages old, but the title leapt from the singer's lips to my mind at that moment in all its appositeness, being born, as I now remember, far more from Haydn and Madame Lehmann than from Shakespeare.

But in most other respects, *The Damask Cheek* provides an exception to the norm of faulty and misty recollection which surrounds a work in its author's mind. Apart from being a collaboration, which means that most of it was talked out instead of thought out, a great deal of it was achieved by correspondence. During the bulk of the period of writing, I was in California, while my collaborator was in New York, so that the letters which we exchanged still exist as a voluminous record from which the story can be told.

Actually, it all began with the Hotel Ansonia in New York City. I was walking up Broadway on a blue and gold morning in late September of last year, when I saw its rococo shape rising before me like something out of my childhood. I did not know what it was, but I had an odd sense that it was somehow important to me, and I decided to go on and find out. I was walking without purpose or direction, trying to think of a play that I might write for Miss Flora Robson, with whom I had spent the evening before. We had been to see Ella Shields, the old-time English vaudeville comedienne and male impersonator, and her singing of "Burlington Bertie from Bow" had sent my mind back to the past in which I had first heard it. The sight of the Hotel Ansonia fixed it there.

I wandered around it and its lobbies, seeing visions of hansoms and the early taxicabs, gentlemen in silk hats and capes squiring ladies with piled hair and satin opera cloaks. I remembered the shiny illustrated advertisements of supper-rooms at London hotels and restaurants in my childhood, and I thought, too, of an aunt of mine, a younger sister of my mother's, who lived in New York and came to visit us each summer, bringing with her what I once heard a movie producer call an "aurora of romance," in her clothes, her jewelry, her Innovation trunks and the touches of American idiom in her speech. Suddenly, the initial idea of *The Damask Cheek* was born in the figure of Miss Robson as an English girl visiting her family of cousins in the New York of a past generation.

Walking home through Central Park I played with this idea, but found myself confronted by a stern difficulty. I have always had a strong disinclination to write of anything with which I have not some personal acquaintance. I am convinced that it would be fatal for me to attempt a play set, for example, in the Orient or on the South African veldt. I did not come to America until 1926; how was I to write of it at an earlier date? On the way back from my walk, however, I stopped in to see my friend, Mr. Lloyd Morris, whom I found working on a book of memories of his own New York childhood, for Mr. Morris is that rarely-met creature, a New Yorker born and bred. He had many times in the past delighted me with tales about an older New York, and I asked him now to tell me something of the Ansonia and its history, whereupon he left his typewriter and obligingly told me stories, until we realized that it was three o'clock and that we had neither of us had any lunch.

Over that belated meal, I suggested the collaboration, on a play for Miss Robson, to which he would especially contribute the detail, color and feeling of a past New York, supplying me with them until I could absorb them and make them my own. For the next month or so we met and talked at least three times a week. The story that we evolved between us was, in its inception, completely different from the plot of *The Damask Cheek*. In the first place, it was set a great deal further back, somewhere between the sixties and the nineties (we were never sure which), and the whole play was of a far more sentimental and dramatic order than the present comedy. We had a "big" situation for the second act, and there was more than a resemblance to *Camille* in what, I suppose, would be called the sub-plot. We both fell in love with a mental picture that we had of Miss Robson, as an American girl, educated in England, and revisiting her country for the first time since childhood, dressed in a costume of the last century, standing at the library window of a house in Washington Square, with a New Year's Day egg-nog party in progress offstage, and watching the snow falling in the Square outside. Of that play and that plot, only the snowstorm now remains.

In November I returned to California and we decided to try to continue our collaboration by correspondence. The first letter in the files comes from me. It is dated Thanksgiving Day, and starts with bad news. I had decided that the play would not do.

"My dear Lloyd," it ran, "I would not dare to write and tell you that the play has gone dead on me again, were it not that I have something else to offer in its stead. But it has, and I have. I took it out for a two-hour walk over the Indian Reservation yesterday morning, and it just won't click into place."

I then proceeded to try and analyze what was wrong, which seemed to me largely that we were concentrating on situation rather than character, and that our principals were entirely passive in the story, having no hand in the shaping of their destinies. In its place, however, a new play had started to form.

"My idea," I wrote, "is to take Miss Robson as a character in a setting and background with which I am familiar—the background of my own childhood and family (if you will give me the New York equivalent thereof), and then to explore that character, rather than try and impose an arbitrarily conceived plot-

xi

formula upon it. For that is really what we have been doing—putting the cart before the horse. How else could we have acted, when I brought you the cart, so to speak, and asked you to help me make a horse? In any case, I, being a writer who cannot invent plot as such, and almost always go wrong when I think I have found a good situation hanging about loose in the air, instead of letting it cocoon itself out of the fibres of character and background that I know and understand, should really have known better.

"So I began again. I saw Flora as the older daughter of some very rich people whom we used to know in England, people who I now think rather patronized my parents. The real ones had three daughters whom I used, as a child, to think dashing and fascinating, until I saw them later through other eyes, when they seemed rather pathetic instead. I saw Flora now at first through the glamourized eyes of a child, and at once the whole thing began to take form, as a study of the girl—a full-length portrait of a girl of thirty, not pretty, but good-natured, humorous, realistic about herself (possibly a sort of female Cyrano in that respect) and accepted generally as a 'good sort.' Indeed, the play, as I see it, might be called 'The Good Sort.' She is the ideal aunt or cousin to the children; rich, good with presents, full of fun, willing to play games with them, and good at dressing up and acting plays with them. It will still be set in period, of course, though I suspect the period may now be about 1912 to make it match with my childhood."

This letter was the beginning of a correspondence that ended by covering about seventy pages of single-spaced typing between us. As the central character grew in my mind, and developed herself on paper between us, so the incidents of the plot began to develop also. The heroine, whom in the earlier play we had planned to call Pauline, known as Polly, now graduated through Ernestine and Ursula to Rhoda Meldrum. She had a good deal more sense of humor than her somewhat melancholy and passive predecessor, especially about herself. Her riches suggested the "buying-off" incident; the discovery that she had a temper of a smoldering and volcanic kind that would erupt, say, once in every seven years, gave birth to the hair-pulling scene in Act Three. Slowly the plot, forming in bits, began to cohere, and to achieve conviction for me because the incidents arose from the character, instead of the character being created to suit incidents.

As the action of the play tightened and arranged itself within the scope of twenty-four hours (as the professors of the drama always advocate), I deluged Mr. Morris with questions. I asked for everything he could tell me about the people; their place and mode of living; their general habits and speech.

"You know the family," I wrote, "partly your own, and partly an American version of what mine was. I see a widowed mother with a son of thirty, possibly two married daughters whom we may or may not meet, and a couple of younger children of, say, sixteen and seventeen. They are the ones who see Rhoda as the glamour girl, remembering her from their visits to England, and being impressed with her Academy portrait by Sargent, and the pictures of her in the English illustrated papers, wearing the gown in which she was presented at Court."

I grew worried over the sleeping arrangements in the house, which it seemed to me I had filled too full for comfort, and wired him asking for indications of who would sleep where. In return, he sent me pages of carefully detailed floor-plans, drawn to scale, showing the entire house with every room, closet and appurtenance, together with copious notes and comments. That is the way I like to work, and I have never been able to write a play without knowing the full offstage lives of all the characters, where they came from when they entered, and where they went to when they left the stage. When we decided that the whole play should revolve around a dance, I asked Mr. Morris for the details of what a private dance in New York of 1909 would be like. Here are some excerpts from his replies:

"The American family that you ask for would live (anywhere from 1900 to 1913) in the East Seventies, or in the Upper East Fifties (like mine) or Sixties. Probably between Madison and Lexington, almost certainly in a brownstone front: no flat—it would still have been considered slightly 'raffish' by conservative, upper-middle-class people of middle age with growing families. . . . Aunt Lucy would not have had a car, and by 1909 would have given up Uncle James's carriage and horses and coachman. In 1909 one *telephoned* to the neighborhood taxi-stand; to go and return from a series of afternoon calls or an evening party, one made a 'rate' with it. . . .

"The dance. Afternoon of the party. The women of the family would have had their nails and hair done by visiting hairdresser and manicure; my family had the two Miss Blanks, who came regularly once a fortnight, and specially for 'events.' They were little spinster sisters who prided themselves on their breeding, and working only for 'the best families'—in which they were wrong, by God! One did hair; the other manicured."

I might interpolate here that the original script of the play contained both these sisters—Miss Jessie and Miss Etta, the former being a manicurist only, and the latter never appearing, but being constantly spoken of. We found, however, after a few performances, that the audience was never able properly to grasp Miss Etta's function or existence; almost every newspaper critic described Miss Jessie as the hairdresser, and we therefore removed her sister entirely, letting Miss Jessie double the roles of manicurist and hairdresser. I was fond of Miss Etta, visualizing her clearly and as of somewhat sterner stuff than her sister, and I was loath to see her go, but that is the theatre. That is also why playwrights sometimes want to write novels.

To return to Mr. Morris's letters:

"Aunt Lucy," he wrote, "would be awfully nervous and fusspot all afternoon. The party, I think, ought to be her idea of doing the proper thing by Rhoda; not 'launching' her, except in an unacknowledged, rather drearily 'Oh-I'll-try' fashion. A caterer (probably Mazetti), would send in potted palms, little gilt chairs, two waiters, and provide *fancy* salads, ices, cakes, *fancy* sandwiches; these would be added to by, possibly, hot bouillon, creamed oysters or lobster Newburg, prepared by cook, split and buttered 'finger-rolls,' a large elaborate cake or tart heavily decorated, probably made by cook. Possibly they might have had a complicated dessert of ice cream, surrounded by tiny eclairs, known as a 'Religieuse,' which figured glamourously in my own childhood. Henri's used to make it. Fifty guests, yes. Carpets up in the downstairs parlor, music room and dining room. Women's cloaks put in Aunt Lucy's bedroom; gentlemen would use (probably) daughter's room and bath, on this occasion, since guest-room is occupied by Rhoda. Younger son would attend, in his first dinner jacket; an event for him!

"Dinner, night of party. No dinner downstairs. Aunt Lucy, Rhoda, and daughter would be served scrambled eggs and bacon, perhaps hot soup, and custard on trays, individually and *early* in their rooms; Jimmy would take younger brother to dine at his club, if he had one, or to near-by hotel; the Netherland, I should think; they would all have had a 'nice, substantial hot lunch' to tide them over, possibly at some downtown restaurant, so as to 'save the servants.'

"You ask where the ladies would shop. Altman's was

the first department store to move 'uptown' to its present location; that would have been about 1908 or 1909, because Knoedler's occupied the 34th and Fifth corner which Altman only added later; Knoedler exhibited a 'sensational' portrait of Mary Garden as 'Thais' by Ben Ali Haggin in the corner window in, I think, 1908 or 1909. Shopping district was Fifth Avenue—Broadway from 23rd to Union Square; 23rd Street between Fifth and Sixth; Sixth Avenue from 23rd to 17th. . . . For household necessities most East Side families used Bloomingdale's, but not for quality goods, except packaged groceries and wines."

(This is the origin of the line which, to my astonishment, has proved one of the biggest laughs in the play.)

"Ladies going downtown to shop often made a 'day' of it; the trip was long, remember—then lunched at Maillard's under the old Fifth Avenue Hotel, or Purcell's (marvelous chicken patties) on the west side of Broadway, about 21st Street."

The above is but a small sample of the richness of detail with which I was inundated over a period of a couple of months, while the play was forming in our heads and on paper. I came to New York again in January, when there were further conversations, and some research from both of us. Colloquialisms of the period were what stumped us both, and were oddly hard to find. I read some plays and novels of the time, and made the interesting discovery that they were seldom written in vernacular. The plays of Clyde Fitch, for example, have almost no trace of Americanism in their locution, save in their lowest-class characters, and might just as well have been written by Sir Arthur Wing Pinero. I re-read *The House of Mirth* and *The Custom of the Country* by Mrs. Edith Wharton, finding them extremely valuable in establishing the changes in social behavior and convention between 1903 and 1913, but from the point of view of idiom they helped very little.

Mr. Morris dug out a few phrases from *Life, Judge* and *Puck,* and listed some of the subjects at which they were poking fun at that period; suffragettes, Fletcherism (a counsel of chewing food thoroughly, presented by Horace Fletcher), the game of Diabolo, the sheath skirt, peek-a-boo shirtwaists, Salome dancers, Christian Science, bridge and airplanes. We searched our own memories and turned up words like "joshing," "spooning," "angelic," "vamoose" and "peachy." I myself excavated, from my own remembrance, the 1909 equivalent of "knowing what it is all about," recalling a magazine alphabet jingle about:

> "Y's a young lady who's highly alive
> To the number of beans that total five."

and remembering a Rhoda of my own childhood who employed it.

I read *Harper's Weekly* for 1909, picking up a few more details, and finally came across one item which, while I longed to include it, I was forced to omit simply because no modern audience would believe that it was anything but a topical gag, which we had invented. I offer it here with an assurance, which I would be unable to give in the theatre, as to its veracity. Motoring was then in its infancy, and the article in question advocated the employment of lightweight drivers. "The heavier the chauffeur," it ran, "the sooner the tires will have to be replaced." I offer this as my personal research contribution to the present rubber situation.

In February I returned to California where I wrote the play alone, mailing it scene by scene to Mr. Morris for comment and correction. The only works of reference that I had by me during the actual writing were a set of English Play Pictorials (in which I found Aunt Lucy's quotation about curls and clusters being considered bad style), Burns Mantle's volumes of *Best Plays,* and *Who's Who in the Theatre.* My discovery that *The Easiest Way* (a play with which I was already familiar) was playing in 1909, was a happy moment, providing me not only an opportunity for some comedy in Michael's clandestine visit (which I gathered was also part of Mr. Morris's experience, just as a forbidden excursion to see Doris Keane in *Romance* in 1916 was part of my own), but also affording me a powerful searchlight on the manners and point of view of the period as regards ladies of the theatre. Without *The Easiest Way,* I would have had a good deal of trouble in establishing the position of Calla in the Randall family.

Watching the play performed, I have been somewhat surprised by the dimensions of the laugh that greets the first mention of *The Easiest Way*. I had not thought that it would be so widely known and recognized by audiences of over thirty years later, even though most people seem to know its famous last line—and to know it wrong. Several persons who read my manuscript challenged my quotation thereof, assuring me that it ought to read "I'm going to Rector's and afterwards to hell," and this, I found, was the caption underneath the photographs of the play in the magazines of the period, although the published version gives the line as we have quoted it in *The Damask Cheek*. I therefore wrote to Miss Frances Starr, who created the role, and now on tour with *Claudia,* asking her if she would mind telling me exactly what it was that she said. Here is her reply:

"That line has trailed me down the years, and now here it is again. I think F.P.A. ran several articles with everyone having a try at it, and it was amazing to read the different versions. It was, as I said it: 'I'm going to Rector's to make a hit—and to hell with the rest.' It is hard to make people believe that the last part of the line was really just a sob, and only just audible.

"Will you please tell me why that play persists in people's minds? I have just had to call a halt here in San Francisco with the men of the press, and assure them that I can really talk about something else. No one seems to think I've ever done anything else. A gen-

tleman appeared at my dressing-room door on Satur-
day, and insisted upon telling me every move I made
in *The Easiest Way* with a nostalgia and memory that
was quite touching, except that I had just had a
matinee and was terribly hungry. The play seems to
be having a renaissance. I feel I really should be getting some crutches, but being one of those irritating
people who has no sense of time, I go blithely on until
some decrepit old lady tells me her governess brought
her to see *The Easiest Way*. Of course I know she is
lying, as governesses didn't take their charges to that
play, and even that doesn't touch me or bring me to
my senses."

The play was finished in April of this year, and sub-
mitted to Miss Robson, who expressed her approval. The
first draft was a good thirty pages too long, owing to the
pleasure we had found in embroidering it with detail
and allusion; and offstage characters like Neil Harding's
mother, Rhoda's two sisters, and Aunt Lucy's two married daughters who lived out West, had to be scraped off
like barnacles, but with more regret. The period of prep-
aration and rehearsal was among the happiest I have
known, and I would like to take this opportunity of
expressing, on behalf of Mr. Morris and myself, our
appreciation of Mr. Raymond Sovey's humorous and
beautifully evocative stage setting, which contributes so
much to whatever veracity the play may have for audiences. Our gratitude to Mr. Wiman for his production is
something which can only be fully appreciated by play-

wrights who have had less fortunate experiences, although I, myself, after ten years of association with him, have come to take his generosity, kindness and understanding almost as a matter of course. I am especially indebted to him now for allowing me my first experience as a director. As for the cast, so beautifully headed by Miss Robson, I can only say (and I hope I am slighting nobody in so doing) that it seems to me to be the best all-round assembly I have had in any of my plays.

My first sight of the Ansonia, and my morning visit to Mr. Morris, have brought us both a degree of pleasure and absorption which it has been a great happiness to hear and see in some measure shared and reflected by the audiences at the Playhouse on 48th Street.

New York City
October, 1942

The Damask Cheek was first presented by Mr. Dwight Deere Wiman at the Plymouth Theatre, Boston, Mass., on Monday, October 5, 1942, and subsequently at The Playhouse, New York City, on Thursday, October 22, 1942, with the following cast:

(In order of appearance)

Rhoda Meldrum	FLORA ROBSON
Miss Pinner	RUTH VIVIAN
Mrs. Randall	MARGARET DOUGLASS
Nora	MARY MICHAEL
Daphne Randall	JOAN TETZEL
Jimmy Randall	MYRON MCCORMICK
Calla Longstreth	CELESTE HOLM
Michael Randall	PETER FERNANDEZ
Neil Harding	ZACHARY SCOTT

Staged by JOHN VAN DRUTEN
Settings and Costumes designed by RAYMOND SOVEY

SCENES

ACT ONE

Afternoon

ACT TWO

SCENE I. Early that evening
SCENE II. Later that evening

ACT THREE

SCENE I. The next morning
SCENE II. The same afternoon

The action takes place in the upstairs living-room of Mrs. Randall's house in the East Sixties, New York City; mid-December, 1909.

ACT ONE

ACT ONE

SCENE: *The library of* MRS. RANDALL'S *house in the East Sixties. New York. Mid-December, 1909.*

The room is on the second floor front. The door to the landing is to the right of the back wall. When it opens, stairs can be seen ascending and descending. The center portion of the back wall is a large alcove, lined with books. It also contains a grand piano with an upholstered piano-bench. The left wall has large windows looking on to the street. The right wall contains double doors leading to MRS. RANDALL'S *dressing room and bedroom. Downstage there is a couch and in front of it a tea-table, set with a filet lace teacloth. In the center, downstage, there is a small chair with arms and an end table beside it. At left another large couch, and behind it a long table on which are some magazines and a candy-dish containing after-dinner mints. Against the back wall in the corner is a table on which are a Tantalus, a siphon and some glasses. Between the windows a writing-desk. There is no ash-tray in the room. The room is good upper-middle class of its period. When the curtain rises, it is late afternoon.*

3

RHODA MELDRUM *is discovered writing letters at the desk. She is an English girl of about thirty, pleasant, good-natured and instantly likeable. She is not pretty, but has what is called a "very sweet face," and is often described as "interesting." There is an expensive quality about her clothes, and her hair is rather elaborately dressed.*

When the curtain rises, MISS PINNER *comes in from* MRS. RANDALL's *dressing room. She is a faded, birdlike little old maid of fifty-odd, dressed in street clothes and hat, and carries a manicuring case. She puts her case and coat down on a chair. She crosses for a magazine and then, catching sight of the back of* RHODA's *head, darts across to her on tiptoe and starts to fidget with her hair.* RHODA *jumps.*

RHODA
(*Starting*)

Oh! Oh, it's you, Miss Jessie.

MISS PINNER

Did I startle you? I'm so sorry! It was just a rebellious tendril. There! (*She moves away*) You have to be a credit to me at the dance tonight, you know. Are you writing home to England?

RHODA

Yes.

MISS PINNER

Giving them all your impressions of America? (RHODA *nods*) It's ten days you've been here now, isn't it?

RHODA
(*Patiently, sealing her letter*)

Yes.

MISS PINNER

Well, now, I won't disturb you. Only don't you go getting ink on your fingers, after I've manicured them so nicely.

RHODA
(*Smiling*)

I won't, Miss Jessie.
(MRS. RANDALL *comes in. She is a woman in the early fifties, gray-haired, handsome, dominant and a little fretful and peevish. She wears a lacy, frilly tea-gown, and carries two florists' boxes of corsage size.*)

MRS. RANDALL

Tea will be brought in a minute. Mazetti's men have just arrived with the gilt chairs and potted palms. (RHODA *rises*) Oh, there you are, dear. What have you been doing?

RHODA
(*Holding up her letter*)

Writing home.

Mrs. Randall

Oh, you are a good girl. Did you give your mother my love?

Rhoda

Of course, Aunt Lucy.

Mrs. Randall

(*Starting to open flowers*)

I'll write to her tomorrow. Well, maybe not tomorrow. But next day.

Miss Pinner

One never wants to do anything the day after a party, I find. Except eat up the sandwiches and things. That's always exciting, to see what's been left over.

Mrs. Randall

Why don't you look in tomorrow, and I'll have Nellie put up some of what's left for *you?*

Miss Pinner

Well, that's very kind of you. If you *have* anything to spare. I know it would be a treat for Mother. (*As* Mrs. Randall *takes out the flowers*) Oh, aren't those beautiful? Lilies of the valley.

Mrs. Randall

They're from the Judge. He knows they're my favorite flower.

6

MISS PINNER

At this time of year, too. They must have cost a small fortune. Have they any odor?

MRS. RANDALL
(*Smelling*)

Very faint.

MISS PINNER
(*Brightly*)

That'll be because they're forced.

MRS. RANDALL
(*Taking up other box*)

I don't know who these can be from. Oh, they're for you, Rhoda.

RHODA

Me? How nice. I wonder who can be sending *me* flowers.

MISS PINNER

You must have made a conquest already.

(NORA, *the maid, enters with tea, which she places on the table.*)

MRS. RANDALL

Oh, here's tea, thank goodness. Is everything all right downstairs, Nora?

NORA

Well, there'll be an awful lot of sweeping up to do, with the dirt they're bringing in on their shoes.

7

MRS. RANDALL

But you've got newspapers down.

NORA

Yes, but they don't keep to the newspapers. (*She goes out.* RHODA *takes out flowers.*)

RHODA

Look, Auntie. Gardenias.

MRS. RANDALL

Who from?

RHODA
(*Reading card*)
"For the Belle of the Ball." From Judge Hazeltine.

MRS. RANDALL
(*Obviously not too pleased*)
Oh, how very kind of him. You must thank him tonight.

RHODA

Of course.

MISS PINNER
(*Archly*)
We'll have to keep an eye on you, or you'll be stealing your aunt's best beau before we know where we are.

MRS. RANDALL

We'd better put both lots in the ice-box till this evening. Would you take them down? I don't want to ring for Nora again. (RHODA *rises*) Or no—no—the ice-box will be so full with all the things for supper. Perhaps if you put them outside the window. I think it's cold enough. (RHODA *crosses to window*) Yes, but not *that* window, dear. Not on the street. Outside *my* window would be better. *Do* you mind? I'm so sorry to make you work like this, but the servants *are* upset.

RHODA

Of course, Aunt Lucy.

MRS. RANDALL

Just put them on the window-sill, and then we'll have our tea.
(RHODA *goes out with flowers.*)

MISS PINNER

She's so nice, Mrs. Randall.

MRS. RANDALL
(*Winding string*)
Yes, it's too bad she isn't pretty.

MISS PINNER

Oh, but it's a very *sweet* face, and *I* think character and disposition are far more important than looks.

9

MRS. RANDALL

Not when it's a question of marriage, I'm afraid.

MISS PINNER
(*Whispering*)

Hasn't she had *any* offers?

MRS. RANDALL

Oh, yes, one or two. You see, there's a lot of money there, so naturally there'd be *some* men, but nothing suitable.

MISS PINNER

Do you think perhaps your sister hoped that over *here* . . . . ?

MRS. RANDALL

Well, I think it was in her mind. Though with a girl of thirty, it's not easy. (RHODA *returns*) Thank you so much, dear. You're a great help. (RHODA *sits behind tea-table*) It isn't snowing, is it?

RHODA

No.

MRS. RANDALL

Oh, good. I've been worrying whether we shouldn't have had the marquee after all. Only it looks so conspicuous.

RHODA

Lemon and one sugar, isn't it, Auntie?

MRS. RANDALL

Yes, dear. Thank you.

MISS PINNER

I'll pass it. (*Rises to do so.*)

RHODA

And you, Miss Jessie?

MISS PINNER

Cream for me, please. Just a little tea, and a lot of cream, and two sugars. Or are they very small?

RHODA
(*Holding up a lump in the tongs*)

Like that.

MISS PINNER

Oh, well, then I think three.
(*Enter* DAPHNE RANDALL, *seventeen and very pretty.*)

RHODA

Daphne, you've got your hair up! You do look nice.

DAPHNE
(*Pleased*)

Do I, really?

RHODA

Very.

MISS PINNER

Quite the young lady, isn't she?

MRS. RANDALL

(*Imperiously*)

Come over here. Let *me* see. Turn around. Yes, that's very satisfactory.

MISS PINNER

I always think it's a great day in a young girl's life, the first time she has her hair up. It's a sort of—milestone!

MRS. RANDALL

(*To* DAPHNE)

Is Calla back?

DAPHNE

Not yet.

MRS. RANDALL

I don't know when *she's* going to get her hair done.

MISS PINNER

Oh, I'll manage.

MRS. RANDALL

Calla's being selfish and thoughtless, as usual.

(*Enter* JIMMY RANDALL. *He is about thirty-two, easy, engaging and rather selfishly casual. He carries a bucket of ice.*)

JIMMY

Hello! Oh, Miss Jessie. (*He sees* DAPHNE *and tweaks
her nose*) Hello, hideous. You've got your hair up.

RHODA

Can I give you some tea?

JIMMY

Well, I played a game of squash after I left the office.
I'd rather have a highball, if nobody minds. . . . This
ice might have been diamonds from the way Nellie tried
to hang on to it.

MRS. RANDALL

Well, she wants all there is for tonight. And why did
you get a bucketful? Two pieces in a glass would have
done perfectly, if you *had* to have ice.

JIMMY
(*Crossing to the drink-table*)

Someone else might like some.

MRS. RANDALL

Who?

JIMMY

Well, Neil's coming in later, before we go to dinner.
He'll want a drink. (*Pours his own.*)

MRS. RANDALL

He isn't here yet, is he? It will have melted by the
time he comes.

MISS PINNER

Is that the handsome Mr. Neil Harding? Have you
seen him yet, Miss Meldrum?

RHODA

I don't think so. Have I, Aunt Lucy? I've met such a
lot of people since I've been here. . . . Who is he?

MRS. RANDALL

He's a friend of Jimmy's. They were in law school at
Harvard together. He lives in Boston. No, you haven't
met him.

MISS PINNER

All the girls are crazy about him. I think even Daphne's
got a teentsy crush on him, if you ask me.

DAPHNE

Oh, Miss Jessie, stop!

RHODA

He sounds a little old for Daphne, if he's Jimmy's
friend.

MRS. RANDALL

He's always been very sweet to Daphne. He used to
take her to the Hippodrome.

DAPHNE
(*Annoyed*)

He took me *once!*

Miss Pinner

(*Coyly*)

I wish he'd taken me!

Rhoda

Well, he sounds exciting. How does such a wonder come to be around loose? I gather he isn't married.

Jimmy

He's had too much sense.

Miss Pinner

Now, Jimmy, that's no talk from an engaged man.

Jimmy

Oh—yes—where is Calla?

Mrs. Randall

I don't know. I haven't seen her since she left us at Maillard's after lunch. She went off on her own some place. Michael went with her. (*Fretfully*) Oh, but you know that. You were there. I don't know when she's going to get her hair done. It's a little inconsiderate of her, keeping everyone waiting like this.

Rhoda

(*Tentatively*)

Perhaps Calla saw it was getting late and decided to have her hair done *out*.

MRS. RANDALL

Oh no, she wouldn't do that!

JIMMY

I brought some flowers for Calla. I gave them to Nellie
to put in the ice-box.

MRS. RANDALL

Oh, you shouldn't have!

JIMMY

Why, what's the matter now?

MRS. RANDALL

Nellie wants the ice-box for other things. You might
have known that!

JIMMY

My God, whose house *is* this? Ours, or the servants'?

MRS. RANDALL

You always think everything should run for your con-
venience. Well, I hope when you're married, you find
things as comfortable as you've been used to. Only, considering that Calla's never run a house in her life . . .
(*She breaks off*) Daphne, run down and get the flowers
out, and put them with the others outside my window.
Or, no, you'd better let Miss Jessie get started on your
nails. It's late. Rhoda, will *you* run down?

JIMMY
(*Protesting*)

Mother!

MRS. RANDALL
Rhoda won't mind. Will you, dear? And just give a look to what's going on.

RHODA
Of course, Aunt Lucy. (*Rises and goes out.*)

MRS. RANDALL
(*Pointedly*)
Have you finished tea, Miss Jessie?

MISS PINNER
(*Gulping it*)
Yes, it was delicious, thank you.

MRS. RANDALL
Well, then, if you could do Daphne now . . .

MISS PINNER
Of course. (*Takes up manicure case*) Come along.

DAPHNE
Can I have polish?

MISS PINNER
I think just for this once we can allow you a soupçon. What do you say, Mrs. Randall?

17

MRS. RANDALL

Well, not too much.

MISS PINNER
(*To* DAPHNE, *as they go*)
Do you remember when you used to *bite* your nails?
(*They disappear.* MRS. RANDALL *rises and replaces
the piano bench, which* DAPHNE *had pulled down-
stage to sit on.*)

MRS. RANDALL
I don't know why you children always have to use this
bench. Surely we have enough furniture.

JIMMY
You know, Mother, you are awful, the way you make
use of Rhoda. She might be a poor relation, instead of
belonging to the one rich branch of our family.

MRS. RANDALL
I don't make use of her.

JIMMY
No more than you would of anybody else, if they'd
let you, I agree.

MRS. RANDALL
(*Hurt*)
Jimmy, that's most unkind of you.

18

JIMMY

I was only kidding. But, honestly, do you think Rhoda's having any kind of a good time here?

MRS. RANDALL

I hope so. I had a tea for her. She's been to the opera, and the theatre—Sothern and Marlowe. Calla took her shopping. She went with Michael to the Bioscope. And the Judge took her to hear Burton Holmes.

JIMMY

Well, maybe that's all she wants.

MRS. RANDALL

I don't know what more I can do. She's not the kind who expects a lot of fuss made over her, fortunately. She's a very sensible girl.

JIMMY
(*Pulling down the bench again*)
Yes, there's never been any nonsense about Rhoda.

MRS. RANDALL

You never were interested in her, were you, Jimmy? *That* way, I mean?

JIMMY

Good God, no!

MRS. RANDALL

I don't see why you shouldn't have been. She's a very nice girl. There's nothing wrong with her.

19

JIMMY

I know, Mother. My trouble is that I've always liked girls—*that* way—who *had* something wrong with them.

MRS. RANDALL

Yes, you have. Oh, I'm not thinking of Calla. You know I'm very fond of Calla. . . .

JIMMY
(*Eagerly*)

You are, aren't you, Mother?

MRS. RANDALL

You know I am.

JIMMY

She and Rhoda seem to get along well together, too.

MRS. RANDALL
(*Unthinkingly*)

Oh, Rhoda gets along with anyone.

JIMMY
(*Laughing*)

That's one of your good ones!

MRS. RANDALL

I didn't mean it like that. (RHODA *returns*) Oh, thank you, dear. No sign of Calla?

RHODA

Not yet.

JIMMY

By the way, Mother, Neil said he wanted to make a—
well, not an announcement exactly, but a sort of little
toast or speech at supper tonight, about Calla and me.

MRS. RANDALL

Oh . . .

JIMMY

After all, we're announcing it tomorrow.

MRS. RANDALL

Yes. I suppose Mr. Harding is the right person.

JIMMY

Well, he'll be my best man. Who else would you sug-
gest?

MRS. RANDALL

No, I—I just wondered if the Judge wouldn't feel it
was his place.

JIMMY

Oh, God, no. We don't want an—oration. This is a
dance, not a funeral.

MRS. RANDALL
(*Plaintively*)

Jimmy, I only said I wondered. You know how fond
he is of you all.

JIMMY

I've never been able to see why that should create an obligation towards people.

(RHODA, *who has settled to some tapestry-work, looks up for a moment.*)

MRS. RANDALL

When you get older, you'll learn to value affection.

JIMMY

I do, if it's mutual. It's just one-sided affection that I can't deal with. I think having people thrust it on you can be the most awful burden. Don't *you*, Rhoda?

RHODA

It's all very well for *you*. You're a man. Men can choose their friends; girls have to take what they can get. If *you* meet someone you like, you can go after them. A poor girl has to wait to be gone after.

JIMMY

Well, Mother didn't think so!

RHODA

What do you mean?

JIMMY

Didn't you know that Mother and Father were never properly introduced?

MRS. RANDALL

Jimmy!

JIMMY

Mother saw him on the beach at Narragansett, thought
he looked attractive, and went straight up and asked him
to take her for a sail. It's true, isn't it, Mother?

MRS. RANDALL

(*Slightly coy*)

Oh, Jimmy! (*To* RHODA) I was seven! And, besides,
our parents knew each other.

JIMMY

Yes, but you didn't find that out till afterwards. You
had no idea he was socially acceptable when you—ac-
costed him.

RHODA

How fortunate that he was. And that they let you
marry. Or where would Jimmy be now?

JIMMY

You mean, what would Jimmy be now? I might have
been a little b——

MRS. RANDALL

(*Interrupting sharply*)

Jimmy, that's enough! I don't like that kind of joke.
And in front of Rhoda, too!

23

JIMMY

Oh, Rhoda knows there are such things as little b——

(RHODA *bends her head over her work to hide her amusement.*)

MRS. RANDALL
(*As before*)

Jimmy, stop it! You're making her blush.

JIMMY
(*Laughing*)

She's not blushing. She's laughing.

(RHODA *looks up. They laugh together.*)

MRS. RANDALL

You two are incorrigible when you get together!

RHODA

I know, Auntie! I'd no idea that you and Uncle James knew each other from childhood.

MRS. RANDALL
(*Sentimentally*)

I always think that's the ideal basis for marriage.

JIMMY
(*Lightly*)

I don't. Where would be the romance in marrying a girl you'd known all your life? Or a girl who'd picked you out for herself?

RHODA
(*Mock-despairingly*)
Yes, that's why the conventions are what they are. It's a man-made world!

JIMMY
(*Rather smugly*)
I guess that's true.

RHODA
Well, you needn't look so pleased about it!

JIMMY
I often think girls must have a rotten time. In *our* set, anyway.

RHODA
(*Briefly*)
They do!

JIMMY
It's different for a girl like Calla, in the theatre. (*He looks at his watch*) Well, I'd better go and start dressing. See you later. (*He goes out.*)

MRS. RANDALL
Tell me, Rhoda, are actresses looked upon the same way in England as they are here?

RHODA
How is that?

MRS. RANDALL
Well, I don't know what the word is, quite—but—

25

when Jimmy first told me Calla was an actress—I was—well—a little worried about it. Perhaps it was unfortunate that I'd been to see *The Easiest Way* only the week before.

RHODA

What is *The Easiest Way?*

MRS. RANDALL

Oh, it's a play that's been a great success. (*She spies the bench and replaces it*) Although a lot of people think it should never have been put on.

RHODA

Oh, then I must see it. Is it really so bad?

MRS. RANDALL

Well, no. It's a very *strong* play, really, if you look at it in the right light. It's all about an actress and her . . . difficulties. Oh, of course I know Calla isn't like that. She's told me all about her life, and how hard it is for a girl to keep straight in the theatre. She says the other girls used to make fun of her, because she *did*—keep straight, I mean. But all the same— And then there are the children—Daphne and Michael. I was very worried about *them,* with Calla, in the beginning.

RHODA

How worried?

26

MRS. RANDALL

I was afraid they might find her romantic or attractive, and get ideas. Of course, she isn't famous or anything. She's never played any parts of consequence. But, all the same—an actress. Fortunately, though, they didn't. They still seem to be more impressed with *you*.

RHODA

With me?

MRS. RANDALL

Oh, you've always been a heroine to the children.

RHODA

I can't imagine why.

MRS. RANDALL

Well, in the first place, they don't know you very well. But they've always remembered you from the times we went to Europe. And then, being English, and seeing your picture in the *Sketch* and *Tatler*. . . . (*Enter* CALLA LONGSTRETH. *She is twenty-two, and very pretty. She wears outdoor clothes, of a kind that in that period might have been regarded as slighty "fast." She carries a small bunch of violets*) Calla, there you are at last! Where have you been?

CALLA

I did some shopping. I brought you these. (*She presents the violets.*)

27

MRS. RANDALL
(*Somewhat nonplussed*)

Oh! That was very nice of you.

CALLA
(*Over-innocently*)

I thought they looked pretty. (*She starts to remove her hat, revealing a very elaborate coiffure, all curls and clusters.*)

MRS. RANDALL

I was wondering what had become of you. (*She looks up and her voice freezes*) You had your hair done.

CALLA
(*Nervously*)

Er . . . Yes, I did.

MRS. RANDALL
(*As before*)

You had it done out?

CALLA

Yes.

MRS. RANDALL

Now, why?

CALLA
(*Vaguely*)

Oh, I don't know. I thought I would.

28

MRS. RANDALL

You knew Miss Jessie was here, waiting for you. Where did you go?

CALLA

The beauty parlor at the Astor. It's where I've been for years.

MRS. RANDALL

Not these last months. What am I going to say to Miss Jessie?

CALLA

Say that I preferred my own place.

MRS. RANDALL

She'll be so hurt. Miss Jessie is a lady. You can't treat her like . . . Did you have your nails done, too?

CALLA

Yes. I'm sorry, Mrs. Randall, but I haven't really liked the way Miss Jessie has been doing me, and I thought as tonight was a special occasion, I'd like to look nice. (*A dead silence. She looks at herself in a mirror*) And I think I do.

MRS. RANDALL

(*Still frigid*)

Well, you know all those curls aren't really fashionable any more, don't you?

CALLA

(*In arms*)

Who says they're not? Miss Jessie?

29

MRS. RANDALL

No. I read it in an English magazine. It said the day of curls and clusters was definitely over, and they weren't good style any more. It's true, isn't it, Rhoda?

RHODA
(*Disclaiming any part of it*)

I really don't know, Aunt Lucy.

CALLA

Well, *I* like it this way.

MRS. RANDALL

Then I suppose there's no more to be said about it. I think you might have told me what you were going to do, that's all, instead of slipping out behind everyone's back. (*Enter* NORA) Yes, Nora, what is it?

NORA

Can I take the tea things?

MRS. RANDALL
(*Chillily*)

Do you want any, Calla?

CALLA
(*Politely*)

No, thank you, Mrs. Randall.

MRS. RANDALL

Very well, then, Nora, you can take them. (NORA *goes out with the tray, returning immediately for the cloth, which* RHODA *has folded for her.* NORA *replaces the tea-table against the downstage right wall*) Calla, what did you do with Michael?

CALLA

He went to a matinee. I left him at Times Square.

MRS. RANDALL

Did you give him the money to go?

CALLA

Yes.

MRS. RANDALL

Well, I wish you hadn't. He goes to quite enough the-atres, as it is, even if it is his vacation. Jimmy's in, by the way. He was asking for you.

CALLA

Oh.

MRS. RANDALL

He's upstairs, dressing.

NORA

Mrs. Randall, the florist's man is asking if you want the hydrangeas banked.

31

MRS. RANDALL

What did you tell him?

NORA

I said I'd ask you.

MRS. RANDALL

Yes, of course I want them banked. They don't look like anything if they're not banked. Oh, dear, how stupid people are, sometimes. I'd better come down.

RHODA

Shall *I* go, Aunt Lucy?

MRS. RANDALL

No, this is something I have to do, myself. If there's one thing I do know about, it's flowers. (*She goes out, followed by* NORA.)

CALLA

(*After her, as the door closes*)

And hair? Did you ever hear such a fuss?

RHODA

I tried to pave the way for you.

CALLA

Not good style. I've heard that about one thing or another ever since I came into this house. Will she be long? Have I time for a highball, do you think?

RHODA

If you're quick.

CALLA

What the hell, anyway? (*Goes to drink-table, and starts to pour herself a small drink*) Did you know that nice girls don't drink whiskey?

RHODA
(*Smiling*)

I think I've heard it.

CALLA

You don't mind all this, do you?

RHODA

All what?

CALLA

This house. This kind of life.

RHODA
(*Shrugging*)

It's what I'm used to.

CALLA

That's not what Jimmy says. He says your home's much sweller than this. Your family's much richer than his, aren't they?

RHODA

A little, perhaps.

33

CALLA

You have a home in the country, as well as your one in London, and it can't really be as stuffy as this. You don't know how this has all got me down. First of all living here, in the house, for three months, till you came, and then being pushed off to that plaguey boarding-house, right around the corner.

RHODA

I'm sorry I turned you out.

CALLA

Oh, it's better than it was here, even if it does close its doors at one in the morning. You know I'm having to sleep here tonight, don't you? I'm sharing your room.

RHODA

Yes, I know.

CALLA

Well, it won't be like this when we're married, and that's going to be sooner than Mrs. Randall thinks.

RHODA

Oh?

CALLA

A year's engagement! Why? I've been on approval for three months. No, just as soon as it's been officially announced—and that'll be tomorrow—then we can go right to it. And if it means a showdown, well, I'm ready for it.

RHODA
(*Warily*)

Is that Jimmy's idea, too?

CALLA

We haven't talked about it, yet. But, listen, if you want to get married, you want to get married. . . .

RHODA

Yes, I see that. But . . . (*Tentatively*) I'd try and do it without the—showdown, did you call it?—with Aunt Lucy.

CALLA

Why?

RHODA

For Jimmy's sake—and your own. He's fond of his mother. . . .

CALLA

Yes, I know he is. I can't think why. She rides him, too, as much as she dares.

RHODA

Well, he's used to her. And if you have a row, that'll mean unpleasantness—and a lot of unhappiness for him. You can manage it tactfully, I'm sure. Why don't you tell her you're sorry about this afternoon?

35

CALLA

Why should I? I already brought her violets!

RHODA

Yes, but I'm afraid she saw through that! But if you say you're sorry, then it'll all be smooth, and we can have a nice time tonight. After all, it's your engagement party.

CALLA

It isn't. She's giving this dance for you.

RHODA
(*Smiling*)

Well, I think she's killing two birds with one stone. And she's gone to a lot of trouble about it.

CALLA

I don't understand you.

RHODA

Why not?

CALLA

Well, I know you're a lot older than me, but you're not *old*. You're Jimmy's age, aren't you?

RHODA
(*Quickly*)

I'm younger than Jimmy.

36

CALLA

Well, all right, then. And you're a good sport, too. Jimmy told me about the time when he got into trouble with that French governess of yours, when he was visiting you in England, and how good you were about it. . . .

RHODA

(*Astonished*)

Jimmy—told you? About that?

CALLA

Sure. Why not? He said you were an awful good scout over the whole thing, when your mother found out about it, and sent her away.

RHODA

Well, Mother took a rather—conventional view of it.

CALLA

And you didn't. That's what I mean. You took his part, then. You're his generation, after all. But you'll go and take his mother's side about a thing like this afternoon, just as though you were his maiden aunt.

RHODA

(*With a touch of suppressed temper*)

I'm not taking anyone's side. I just said I thought it would be nice if you'd—well, not apologize—because it isn't as important as that—but if you'd say you were

37

sorry you'd hurt her feelings, or been thoughtless. I just thought it might make it pleasanter all round, for everybody. But if you don't want to, it really doesn't matter a damn.

CALLA

There's no need to get mad.

RHODA
(*Snappishly*)
I'm not in the least mad!

CALLA

All right. I'll say I'm sorry. I feel good this afternoon, anyway. I went to a fortune teller. She told me wonderful things.

RHODA

What did she tell you?

CALLA

She told me I was going to get a lot of money very soon. From somewhere quite unexpected.

RHODA
(*Smiling. Calm again*)
Well, that's nice!

CALLA

She said nothing that I'd planned was going to work out the way I'd planned it, but that it was all going to

38

be peachy. And she saw the letter R. She saw it all over everything.

RHODA

Well, it *will* be all over everything, won't it?

CALLA

How do you mean?

RHODA

Well, your linen and everything. It'll be your initial when you're married.

CALLA

Oh, that's right, too. I never thought of that. Wasn't that clever of her? Do you go to fortune tellers?

RHODA

Now and then.

CALLA

Have any of them ever told you anything that came true?

RHODA

No, not yet. They're always predicting marvelous things, but they're never going to happen for ages. An astrologer I went to told me that this was going to be my good year.

CALLA

Has it been?

RHODA

Not particularly, so far.

39

CALLA

Well, you haven't got much of it left.
(MRS. RANDALL *returns*.)

MRS. RANDALL

I really think I shall have to get rid of Nellie, after this party. What are you drinking, Calla?

CALLA
(*After a second*)

Just some charged water, Mrs. Randall. (*She replaces the glass.*)

MRS. RANDALL

Oh, I see.

CALLA

I'd better get back to my boarding-house.

MRS. RANDALL

I wish you'd remember to call it a hotel.

CALLA

Why?
(RHODA *looks up, fearful of another scene starting.*)

MRS. RANDALL

Because it *is* a hotel. And it *sounds* nicer. Don't be back any later than nine o'clock, will you?

40

CALLA

Jimmy said he was going to call for me on his way from dinner with Neil Harding.

MRS. RANDALL

Well, then, I'll tell him. I'd like you all here by nine.

CALLA

What time are the guests coming?

MRS. RANDALL

They're asked for ten. I don't suppose there'll be anyone here before half-past, though.

CALLA

Well, what do we do from nine o'clock, then?

MRS. RANDALL
(*Wearily*)

Calla, I wish you wouldn't argue. If you don't want to be here at nine, say so.

(RHODA *exchanges a warning glance with* CALLA.)

CALLA

I'll be here. And—I'm sorry if I annoyed you about the hairdresser.

MRS. RANDALL

You didn't annoy me. If you'd told me what you were going to do . . .

CALLA

I know. It was thoughtless of me. I'm sorry.

MRS. RANDALL

All right.

CALLA

(*With a glance at* RHODA)

Well, good-bye, then.

MRS. RANDALL

Good-bye, Calla. (CALLA *goes out*) Did you tell her to apologize to me?

RHODA

No, of course not, Aunt Lucy.

MRS. RANDALL

You did. She's never apologized before without somebody prompting her to it. Usually Jimmy. (*Rises and crosses to drink-table where she takes up* CALLA's *glass and smells it*) I thought so. Whiskey.

RHODA

Isn't that Jimmy's glass?

MRS. RANDALL

(*Taking up the other dirty glass and smelling that, too*)

They're both the same. You see. Deceitful.

RHODA

Oh, Aunt Lucy.

MRS. RANDALL
(*Coming and sitting beside* RHODA)
Oh, Rhoda, I'm so worried. I've *prayed* that something would happen to stop it before it was too late. That's why I insisted on this three months' trial, and on her living here. I hoped that if Jimmy saw her in his own surroundings, he might realize—how unsuitable it was.

RHODA
Jimmy doesn't know you don't approve?

MRS. RANDALL
No. No. It was obvious that he was very—infatuated with her, and he isn't a boy to brook opposition. And since his father died . . . (*She breaks off, tearfully*) But it's been a dreadful strain pretending I was fond of her and pleased about it. I've pretended to everyone. Oh, why couldn't Jimmy have wanted to marry *you*? (RHODA *laughs*) Why do you laugh? I think you'd be an ideal daughter-in-law.

RHODA
(*Laughing*)
Oh, no, I wouldn't. You don't really know me a bit, Aunt Lucy. I'm awful, underneath.

MRS. RANDALL
I don't believe that. You seem to me to have all the

43

right qualities for Jimmy. You'd make a wonderful mother. You're very good style. You're sensible, practical, good-tempered. . . .

RHODA

That's where you're wrong, Auntie. I've got a filthy temper when I let go. Don't you remember how I cut poor little Lily Mandeville's head open just in a quarrel in the nursery?

MRS. RANDALL

That was when you were tiny.

RHODA

(*Lightly*)

I still get impulses that way.

MRS. RANDALL

So does everyone. The trouble with you is that you're *too* good-natured. At least, that's what your mother says.

RHODA

Yes, she's talked to me about it.

MRS. RANDALL

You know, *men* like a little mystery in a girl.

RHODA

Well, I think it's a bit late for me to manage that.

MRS. RANDALL

We'll have to see what we can do.

RHODA

Aunt Lucy, did Mother send me over here for you to find someone for me?

MRS. RANDALL

Of course not. She thought it was a little lonesome for you at home, with both your sisters married, and all the girls you came out with, too. She said you were spending all your time with married couples and suffragettes. Naturally, she'd like to see you married. And in a new country, where nobody knows you . . .

RHODA
(*Teasingly*)

You think I might seem more mysterious? The way French actresses always succeed in England, no matter how bad they are?

MRS. RANDALL
(*Offended*)

Of course, if you're going to make fun of the whole thing . . .

RHODA

Well, that's better than taking it too seriously, don't you think? (*Taking her hand*) I'm all right, Aunt Lucy. I'll surprise you all yet.

MRS. RANDALL

Well, you haven't a great deal of time.

(JIMMY *returns. He wears tails and white tie and carries a cocktail shaker and ingredients.*)

JIMMY

Haven't a great deal of time for what?

MRS. RANDALL
(*Embarrassed*)

What did you say, Jimmy?

JIMMY

I said what hasn't Rhoda a great deal of time for?

RHODA

To get dressed.

JIMMY

Well, good God, you've got about two and a half hours. *You*'re not going out to dinner. By the way, Michael's not back. He'd better hurry, if he's coming with us.

MRS. RANDALL

Yes, you'll have to tie his tie for him. (*To* RHODA) It's Michael's first dinner jacket. (*Back to* JIMMY) And don't let him drink anything at dinner. He can have some champagne tonight. Just a glass, but that's all.

JIMMY

Oh, talking of that, what is that stuff I saw down-stairs?

MRS. RANDALL

What stuff?

JIMMY

Well, it's supposed to be champagne. Where on earth did you get it?

MRS. RANDALL

I got it at Bloomingdale's. It's very good and very reasonable.

JIMMY

That's not possible.

MRS. RANDALL

Why isn't it?

JIMMY

Because champagne is something that can't be good *and* reasonable.

MRS. RANDALL

It's quite good enough for an occasion like tonight. Nobody ever notices what they drink at a dance! (*She goes out, into her bedroom.*)

JIMMY

Well, I think I'll bring a couple of bottles of decent stuff up here, for those who do notice. And what do you say we keep this as a sitting-out room, just for *us*?

47

RHODA

Fine. (*She starts for the door.*)

JIMMY

What are you running away for? You don't have to go yet. Stay and talk to me.

RHODA
(*Returning*)

All right.

JIMMY

Mind if I smoke?

RHODA

Of course not.

JIMMY

Will you?

RHODA

No, thanks. (*She resumes her tapestry.*)

JIMMY

By the way, everything is all right, isn't it? We weren't caught, were we?

RHODA
(*With a glance over her shoulder*)

No. I got back on the stroke of four, just in time for Miss Jessie. Aunt Lucy asked me where I'd been. . . .

JIMMY

And you said Altman's . . .

RHODA

Well, that was true. I didn't have to lie, like you.

JIMMY

What do you mean?

RHODA

You said you played squash after you left the office—
not after you left *me*.

JIMMY

Well, it *was* after I left the office. I left the office at
lunch-time. You haven't really got a conscience about it,
have you?

RHODA
(*Smiling*)
Not really. I just feel I've had an adventure.

JIMMY

Well, if going skating at the St. Nicholas Rink for an
hour with *me,* is an adventure, I feel sorry for you.

RHODA

Oh, but it was—for me.

JIMMY
(*Waving a dead match, and looking around*)
I must remember to bring an ash-tray up here for
tonight. (*He drops the match in the wastebasket*) I en-

joyed this afternoon, too. And we never would have had it, if Mother hadn't dragged me uptown to take you all to lunch. You know, it's extraordinary how she hates going anywhere without a man.

RHODA

Well, that's her generation.

JIMMY
(*Trying a Cockney accent*)

Ow, jest a pore, weak, unprotected femyle, eh? (*Sitting beside her*) How's that for Cockney, after all these years?

RHODA

Not bad.

JIMMY

Do some real Cockney for me.

RHODA
(*In perfect Cockney*)

Oh, Mr. Randall, you mustn't blame your poor old Mum for likin' to 'ave a man around. It's only nacheral; it is, reelly. We women are like that, you know—frail and 'elpless. I'm ever such a timid little thing, myself.

JIMMY
(*Still in Cockney*)

Is that what makes you do this mouldy tapestry?

RHODA
(*Cockney*)

Oh, you're barmy! It's beautiful. It's ever such good taste.

JIMMY
(*Cockney*)

Well, you might put it away while *I'm* talking to you. (*He grabs it.*)

RHODA
(*Slapping his hand away*)

Why?

JIMMY
(*Cockney*)

Oh, I 'ates to see you doing it. It looks so—old-maidish and respectable.

RHODA
(*Still Cockney*)

Well, I *am* respectable! And as for being an old maid, I'll thank you not to throw that up against me. I've 'ad me chances, let me tell you. (*Then, in her own voice*) You don't mean you *really* hate this, do you?

JIMMY

Well, it does look a bit settled and dreary. You're having a pretty dreary time here, aren't you? I wish I could do something about that—but with Calla . . .

RHODA

Of course. I know.

JIMMY

Don't you ever feel the urge to—break out?

RHODA

(*Fiercely*)

Yes. Quite often!

JIMMY

But you never do. Why not?

RHODA

Because there wouldn't be any point in it, except for the sheer satisfaction of having done it—*once*. Like a kind of wild oat.

JIMMY

I believe in wild oats. Moderately wild.

RHODA

I know you do. There was Thérèse. *She* was moderately wild.

JIMMY

I didn't mean that! That was a fine to-do, wasn't it? Your mother was awful about it. Opening letters and . . . I suppose I ought to be ashamed of all that.

RHODA

Oh, I don't know. I don't think Thérèse was exactly an innocent girl.

JIMMY

I know damn well she wasn't. You were a grand scout over that.

RHODA

I gather you've told Calla all about it.

JIMMY

Oh, sure. Calla likes to hear about my adventures. It's funny.

RHODA
(*Chaffing him a little*)
But you like telling about them, don't you?

JIMMY

Stop kidding me. I'm not a ladies' man, really.

RHODA
(*As before*)
No?

JIMMY

Not the way Neil is, for example.

RHODA

Neil? Oh, the fascinating Mr. Harding.

JIMMY

Neil's always knee-deep in half a dozen affairs at the same time. Girls fall for him so violently and throw themselves at him.

53

RHODA

And he always picks them up?

JIMMY

Well, he takes what the Gods give. Say, how about my mixing a little cocktail before he gets here? Will you have one?

RHODA

Yes, I'd like to.

JIMMY

That's the girl. (*Goes to the drink-table.*)

RHODA

You know, you're all making me very curious about Mr. Harding. I can hardly wait.

JIMMY

Oh, I don't think he's your type. Or you his.

RHODA

Why not?

JIMMY

Oh, he likes vamps and sirens, really. Mysterious, enigmatic, smouldering women.

RHODA

In the intervals of taking what the Gods give, you mean?

JIMMY

There used to be a Roumanian girl. That was a great affair. (*A tiny pause*) Why do I talk to you like this?

RHODA

I don't know. Why do you?

JIMMY

Search me. You don't mind, do you?

RHODA
(*Quietly*)

Not at all. (*There is a moment's pause*) Do you mind if I ask you a very impertinent question? You needn't answer if you don't want to.

JIMMY

What is it?

RHODA

Do you intend to go on—sowing wild oats after you're married?

JIMMY

Good Lord, no. Why?

RHODA

I just wondered.

JIMMY

No, I believe in putting that kind of thing completely

55

behind one. Where would be the point in getting married, otherwise?

RHODA

I agree.

JIMMY
(*Handing the cocktail*)
Well—having disposed of that question—here's how!
(*They drink*) It's funny, having you here. You know, coming in here this afternoon, and finding you behind the tea-table, reminded me so much of England and your place down in Hatfield. I felt I was right back there. We did have fun, didn't we?

RHODA

Yes.

JIMMY
It's strange, you know, that all of that appeals to me so much. It's not the kind of life I'll ever lead. It's not Calla's dish, by any means.

RHODA

No, I suppose not.

JIMMY
(*Bringing down the bench again*)
And that's funny, too. Calla, I mean. She's the last sort of girl I'd ever have imagined myself marrying. I always thought I'd marry—oh, a sort of girl of good family—one of Boston's best—someone like Neil's sister.

56

RHODA

What's she like?

JIMMY
(*Reflectively*)

Well—she's not exactly pretty, but she's—good style. Sensible, practical—you know, not a bit mysterious, or anything. . . .

RHODA
(*Parenthetically*)

Poor girl!

JIMMY
(*Continuing*)

But she's a wife that anyone would be proud of. You know, living in the country and having slews of kids. I've always wanted kids. . . .

RHODA

Yes, you ought to have them. You've always been good with children. Is—Calla fond of children?

JIMMY
(*Slowly*)

I don't really know. I don't think, very. (*Then quickly*) Well, as I say, that's what I'd always seen myself marrying. But when it came to falling in love . . . Well, I guess there's some kind of a streak in me that makes me fall for girls who are a bit—tarnished. No, I don't mean that. That's a hell of a thing to say.

57

RHODA

I know what you mean. You've always been like that.
When you were small you always used to like—sparkly
things. There was a children's fancy-dress party we gave
in Cumberland Terrace, and you were frightfully fasci-
nated by a girl in a dress all made out of tinsel. You followed her about all the evening.

JIMMY

Good Lord, yes, I remember. And you were . . . ?

RHODA
(*Grimly*)

A snowflake.

JIMMY

What was the tinsel girl's name?

RHODA
(*Awkwardly*)

Er—Lily Mandeville.

JIMMY

Yes, you had a fight with her about something, didn't
you? Blonde and very pretty, wasn't she?

RHODA
(*Sharply*)

No, she wasn't. She was almost cross-eyed. It was just

her dress. You like things with a showy wrapping. (*She picks up her work again.*)

JIMMY

Tinsel, in fact. (*Pointing*) Tinsel versus tapestry.

RHODA

By the way, I'm making this as a footstool for Grandma Meldrum. She's an old lady now, and I'd hate to disappoint her. So—may I be allowed to finish it?

JIMMY

Well, I remember she gave me a five-pound note once; so for her sake . . . (*Enter* MICHAEL, *aged sixteen*) Oh, you've come in, have you? Have you forgotten we're supposed to be taking you out to dinner?

MICHAEL

Am I late?

JIMMY

It's twenty to seven. Where have you been?

MICHAEL

To a matinee. I waited at the stage door afterwards. Then I walked home. I'm sorry I'm late.

JIMMY

What did you see?

MICHAEL

You won't tell Mother?

JIMMY
(*Amused*)

What have you been up to now?

MICHAEL

I went to *The Easiest Way*.

JIMMY
(*As before*)

Did you? Did you like it?

MICHAEL

Yes, it was wonderful.

JIMMY

Well, you'd better start dressing. (*To* RHODA) I think I'll go and rout out that champagne, and put it on ice. Don't forget tonight the good stuff will be up here. (*He goes.*)

MICHAEL

You won't tell Mother, either, will you, Rhoda? She told me I wasn't to go, but . . .

RHODA
(*Smiling*)

Of course.

MICHAEL

It's wonderful, really. It's all about an actress who . . .

RHODA

Michael, I don't think you've time to tell me the story now.

MICHAEL

All right. I'll tell you later. Has anybody told you the last line?

RHODA

No. What is it?

MICHAEL

Oh, it's no good unless you know the whole plot. But it's that that shocks people. There was quite a gasp when she said it this afternoon. *You* ought to see it.

RHODA

Well, I like a good gasp in the theatre.

MICHAEL

Maybe it wouldn't shock *you*. You're so sort of— sophisticated and Bohemian.

RHODA
(*Surprised*)

Me?

MICHAEL

Yes.

RHODA

Goodness!
(DAPHNE *comes in.*)

DAPHNE

Oh, you're back.

MICHAEL
(*Gesturing coiled hair*)

Well, look at *you!*

DAPHNE

Where did you go?

MICHAEL

Wouldn't you like to know?

DAPHNE

Did you go to a theatre?

MICHAEL

Maybe. I must go and put on my dinner jacket. (*He goes out.*)

DAPHNE
(*Calling after him*)

All right, I don't want to know! (*To* RHODA) Where *has* he been?

RHODA

To a matinee. He'll tell you. (*Pause*) Daphne, I found something on the stairs this afternoon. A poem. I think you must have dropped it. (*She takes it from her waist-band*) Here. (*She hands it.*)

DAPHNE
(*Blushing scarlet*)

Thank you.

RHODA

It is yours?

DAPHNE

Yes. I must have dropped it out of my book. Thanks. (*She turns to go, overcome with embarrassment.*)

RHODA

Daphne.

DAPHNE
(*Stopping, poised for flight*)

What?

RHODA

Can I talk to you a minute?

DAPHNE

What about?

RHODA

I read that poem. No one else has seen it, have they? (DAPHNE *shakes her head*) Is that just something you've made up, or is it true?

DAPHNE

It's true.

63

RHODA

I thought it was. You really feel like that about someone? (DAPHNE *nods*) And he doesn't—care for you?

DAPHNE

No.

RHODA

Is it—Mr. Harding?

DAPHNE

How did you guess?

RHODA

I guessed—this afternoon, when they were talking
about him.

DAPHNE

You don't think *they* . .

RHODA

No.

DAPHNE

Well, what made *you* . . . ?

RHODA

Oh, I don't know. Perhaps because I'm nearer your
age, and—remember what it feels like. He doesn't know
you feel like that about him?

DAPHNE

I used to think he did. . . . That time he took me to

the Hippodrome. . . . It was the most wonderful afternoon I've ever spent. We went to tea at the Plaza afterwards, and it was awful because all the time I kept thinking how little more of it there was left, and that spoiled
it so much that I couldn't really enjoy it. He always said
he'd take me out again—but he never did. He was just
being kind, that time. To Jimmy's kid sister.

RHODA

Are you really unhappy about him?

DAPHNE

I've been unhappy—only sort of happily unhappy, if
you know what I mean. . . .

RHODA

I do.

DAPHNE

I mean, it's all right, if you know there's no chance.
You can sort of accept that, and almost—well—enjoy it.
I mean, if I thought that he was in love with someone
else, for instance. Well, I could stand that—and feel like
Viola in *Twelfth Night,* or something. You know . . .

RHODA
(*Nodding*)

"She never told her love . . ."

DAPHNE

"But let concealment, like a worm i' the bud . . ."

65

RHODA

"Feed on her damask cheek."

DAPHNE

Yes, but it seems he isn't in love with anyone. He's just an awful ladies' man. Makes love to every girl he meets. . . . Well, that makes it all different. I mean, why shouldn't he be interested in *me,* then?

RHODA

You're a little young for him, aren't you?

DAPHNE

I don't think it's that. I think the trouble is that he still thinks of me as a kid, the way he first knew me. I believe men get an idea of you as one thing, and then never can see you any different.

RHODA
(*With a laugh*)

Daphne, you're much too young to generalize about men. (DAPHNE *is hurt*) I don't mean to laugh at you. And actually I think you're quite right. Men do—get an idea of you as one thing. But you're only eighteen.

DAPHNE

You mean I'll get over it?

RHODA

Of course you will.

66

DAPHNE

Did you have anything like this happen to you? When you were my age?

RHODA

Yes.

DAPHNE

Was it the same? Was he a lot older than you?

RHODA

No. Not a lot.

DAPHNE

Well, why didn't you get married, then?

RHODA

He didn't think of me that way.

DAPHNE

Was he—wonderful?

RHODA
(*With a smile*)

I don't know. No, not in the sense you mean, I think.

DAPHNE

What was he like?

RHODA

Oh, he was sweet, and selfish, and jolly, and sort of —dependent. Though *he* never thought he was. He

67

was very good at games, and wonderful with children. I think he was the sort of man who never quite grows up, himself, and that's always the hardest kind to get over.

DAPHNE

But you did get over it?
(JIMMY *returns, with* NEIL HARDING. NEIL *is about* JIMMY'S *age, and very handsome.*)

JIMMY

Neil's been here about ten minutes. Upstairs, talking to Michael.

NEIL

They told me you were up there. Hello, Daphne.

DAPHNE

Hello.

NEIL

I haven't seen you for ages.

JIMMY

Oh, Rhoda, you don't know . . . I'm sorry. This is Mr. Harding. My cousin, Miss Meldrum.

RHODA

How do you do? (*Holds out her hand.*)

68

NEIL
(*Taking it*)

How do you do? I've just been hearing a lot about you from Michael.

JIMMY
(*To* RHODA)

That's unfortunate for you!

NEIL

Not at all. He painted a most dashing portrait.

RHODA
(*To* JIMMY)

See?

JIMMY

Michael's prejudiced. She took him to Rumpelmayer's in London when he was seven, and let him eat himself sick with cream cakes. Memories like that color a whole lifetime. Now, *my* earliest memories of Rhoda are getting a black eye, a nosebleed, and sharing our first cigarette.

NEIL

Weren't *you* sick?

JIMMY

We were sick—together. That's what makes the difference.

RHODA
(*Lightly*)

So you see, I haven't much to hope from Jimmy.

JIMMY
(*Putting a brotherly arm around her shoulder*)
But we've been very good friends, all the same!

RHODA
(*Smiling at him*)
Memories that color a whole lifetime.

JIMMY
(*Smiling back*)
Sure! (*He leaves her, moving away to put his cigarette ash in the wastebasket. Her eyes follow him for just a moment too long.*)

NEIL
(*Opening his cigarette case*)
May I be allowed to smoke?

RHODA
(*Catching herself, and bringing her attention back to him with a start*)
Oh, of course.

NEIL
Will *you?* Michael tells me that you do. Still do, I should say, after Jimmy's story.

RHODA
(*Smiling*)
Thank you. (*She takes a cigarette*) Michael seems to have told you a great deal.

70

NEIL

Well . . . (*He lights her cigarette for her.*)

RHODA

You know, Mr. Harding, I've heard a lot about *you,* too—from Jimmy.

NEIL

Also a dashing portrait, I hope?

RHODA

(*Smiling*)

Oh, yes, quite. (*She glances at* JIMMY, *and then back again at* NEIL) *Quite!*

CURTAIN

ACT TWO

ACT TWO

Scene I

Scene: *The same. About nine o'clock the same evening.*

Michael, *seated on the bench, and wearing a rather inexperienced dinner jacket, is in the middle of a long recital to* Rhoda, *who is working on her tapestry. She wears a quite beautiful evening gown.*

Michael
(*Very earnestly*)
No, she's not *bad,* exactly; she's just *weak.* She does try to give up the old life for him, but she's been sapped by luxury. That's what the other man tells him in the first act. He says, "Her simplest gown flirts with a hundred-dollar note." (*Breaking off*) Do dresses really cost that much?

Rhoda
A hundred dollars? That's twenty pounds. Some, yes. Smart ones. You can get them for less.

Michael
So, you see, she never mails the letter. She just burns it. It's the Easiest Way.

75

Rhoda

Yes, I see.

Michael

Well, then . . . (*He breaks off, as* Daphne *comes in from the dressing room. She wears a very ingenue evening gown*) What do you want?

Daphne

Mother says it's after nine, and are you quite sure they were coming right over?

Michael
(*Irritably*)

They said they were. They were just going to call for Calla.

Daphne

Well, Mother says will you telephone the hotel, and see if they've left?

Michael

Why can't you do it?

Daphne

Why should I?

Michael

Because I'm telling Rhoda something.

Daphne

What?

MICHAEL

None of your business. Oh, Daph, vamoose!

DAPHNE

I won't. I've just as much right here as you have. And one of your studs has come out. (*She sits down.*)

RHODA

(*With a gesture of her head*)
Daphne, be a good girl, and go and telephone.
(MICHAEL *attends to the stud.*)

DAPHNE

Oh, all right. (*To* MICHAEL) If you'd asked me properly . . . (*She goes out.*)

RHODA

Now, go on.

MICHAEL

Where was I?

RHODA

At the end of the second act.

MICHAEL

Oh, yes. Well, then in the next act, they're living together again, and it's all rich and everything, and a telegram comes to say that John's coming back.

77

RHODA
(Pretending excitement)

Oo!

MICHAEL

Well, then she's going to confess everything to him, only the other woman comes—the other—(*Choosing the lesser word*)—actress. And she says that she's a fool to tell him. She says that all men lie to women, and that women like them are just the common prey of any man who comes along. She says that . . .

RHODA
(Interrupting)

Look, Michael, I don't think you'd better go into all the dialogue now. Your mother will be in, any minute. Just tell me the story.

MICHAEL

Oh, well, then John comes and he wants her to marry him and go to Nevada with him that afternoon. He still thinks she's reformed, and he's reformed, too.

RHODA

What's he reformed from?

MICHAEL

Oh, he used to be sort of wild, but he says being in love with her has cured him. He says she's made him believe in God. Well, after that, she just can't tell him. . . .

RHODA

No, I can see that.

MICHAEL

Only Brockton comes in—and he's got a latch key, and it's *her* apartment, so then John *knows!* Well, then there's a terrific scene where he tells her that she isn't any good. (*With some relish*) He says she's not immoral, she's un-moral, and that with her it's the easiest way, and she'll just sink down and down to the very bedrock of depravity. So she says she'll shoot herself. She gets the revolver, and everything, and he just stands there and dares her to do it, and she can't. So he goes away, and she's left all alone. And that's when it comes. The last line, I mean. She tells the maid to get out her prettiest dress. She says, "Dress up my body and paint my face. They've taken my soul away with them." And the maid asks her if she's going out, and she says, "Yes, I'm going to Rector's to make a hit, and—(*Dropping his voice*)— to hell with the rest." I think she means she going to become a—well, a professional. And that's the end. It's wonderful. Oh, my stud's gone again. (*He busies himself with it.*)

RHODA
(*Amused*)
Well, you've had an afternoon, haven't you?

MICHAEL
It's awfully stark and true to life.

RHODA
(*Smiling*)
What makes you think that?

MICHAEL
Well, Jimmy's talked to me—about life, and about Calla, and how hard it is for a girl to go straight on the stage. The other women—and the men who prey on them, and lead them astray. Rhoda, you don't think . . .

RHODA
What?

MICHAEL
Well, after the play this afternoon, I was sort of thinking about it, and you don't think that Calla could be like the girl in it, do you? And that she's marrying Jimmy to sort of get back?

RHODA
(*Really rather shocked*)
No, of course I don't. Michael, what absolute nonsense! Jimmy and Calla are in love with each other.

MICHAEL
The girl was in love with the man in the play. And he with her. That's why she was afraid to tell him the truth. I mean, if Calla had been—if there had been something . . .

80

RHODA

(*Sharply*)

Michael, stop it. I don't want to hear any more about it. I agree with everybody who has said it's a very improper play, and you ought never to have seen it!

MICHAEL

Well, I never thought you'd say that! I was only telling Neil this evening how broad-minded you were.

RHODA

Well, I'm not broad-minded when it comes to you suspecting things about your future sister-in-law. And what made you tell him that, anyway?

MICHAEL

He was asking what you were like.

RHODA

And a fine picture you seem to have painted!

MICHAEL

He said he thought you sounded fascinating.
(*Enter* MRS. RANDALL *from the dressing room. Full evening dress; black velvet and old lace.*)

MRS. RANDALL

Well, what did they say?

MICHAEL

Who?

MRS. RANDALL

When you telephoned.

MICHAEL

Oh—Daph's doing it now.
 (*Re-enter* DAPHNE.)

DAPHNE

They'd just left.

MRS. RANDALL

Oh, good. Well, now . . . (*Breaking off*) Michael,
what are you fidgeting with your shirt like that for?

MICHAEL

The stud won't stay in.

MRS. RANDALL

Let me see. No, you've broken the buttonhole. Now,
how did you do that?

MICHAEL

Pushing it through.

MRS. RANDALL

You're not supposed to push them through. Those
studs unscrew.

MICHAEL

Well, I tried unscrewing them, but the top kept dropping off. I stepped on one of them. I think I bent it.

MRS. RANDALL

Michael, those studs were your father's! I'd never have given them to you, if . . . Really, you're not fit to have decent things!

MICHAEL

I couldn't help it.

MRS. RANDALL

Well, you can't wear it like that. You'd better go and change your shirt. You've got another. I bought you two. And don't try putting the studs in yourself this time. Get Jimmy to help you.

MICHAEL

That's going to mean tying my tie again. It took him hours before.

MRS. RANDALL

Michael, stop fussing, and do as I tell you. (MICHAEL goes. MRS. RANDALL *pounces on the bench again, replacing it*) Oh, and Daphne, Miss Jessie's staying on to listen to the toasts and speeches tonight. She's resting in your room till supper time, as mine is wanted for the wraps. So don't disturb her.

83

DAPHNE

How's she going to get home?

MRS. RANDALL

She'll have to have a taxicab. Michael can go with her
to see she gets there all right. Now I must go down and
see what's happened to the band.

DAPHNE

They're here. But they haven't got "Yip-I-Addy-I-Aye."

MRS. RANDALL

Oh, dear. If it isn't one thing, it's another. (*She goes
out.*)

DAPHNE

I do think your dress is angelic. I wonder if I'll ever
have a Paris frock. I hate this thing. It's so young.

RHODA

You look very nice. You're very pretty, you know,
Daphne.

DAPHNE

Do you think so? I think I look like the girls on candy
boxes. No character.

RHODA

Well, that's the type men like.

DAPHNE

You don't mean to say they don't like *you*?

RHODA

Oh, yes, they *like* me. That's the trouble.

DAPHNE

I've always thought you were the type that they'd find fascinating. Elegant and poised. I told Neil you were.

RHODA

When?

DAPHNE

Oh, a long time ago, when he saw your picture in your gown when you were presented at Court. You know, I always thought you'd marry someone like an ambassador to St. Petersburg, or somewhere, and give receptions at the head of a great staircase, all in diamonds, with a huge white feather fan.

RHODA

Well, that's a very flattering picture.
(*Enter* JIMMY, NEIL *and* CALLA. CALLA *wears a rather extreme evening gown.*)

JIMMY

Well, here we are.

RHODA

Did you see Aunt Lucy? She was worrying about you.

JIMMY

Calla kept us waiting.

CALLA
(*Sitting*)

Yes, and now we are here, what do we do? Sit and twiddle our thumbs?

JIMMY

Well, I should think we might all have a little drink. (*Goes to drink-table, where there is now champagne in a bucket*) Yes, this is good and cold.

NEIL

Isn't it a bit soon after dinner for champagne?

CALLA

Well, we've got to do something.

NEIL
(*Flippantly*)

How about a nice parlor game? Or a little music?

DAPHNE

Rhoda plays. She sings, too.

NEIL
(*To* RHODA)

Does she?

RHODA

Not seriously.

DAPHNE

She does, too. Why don't you sing, Rhoda?

RHODA

No, Daphne.

NEIL

What do you sing?

JIMMY

She used to sing a ballad called "Melisande in the Wood."

RHODA

Jimmy, I'll kill you.

JIMMY

You did, too.

RHODA

You used to recite "Little Boy Blue," but I'm not bringing that up against you.

JIMMY

I'll do it now, if you'll sing "Melisande in the Wood." Come on. (*Starting to overact the song*) "Lean down, lean down, to the water, Melisande."

CALLA

Oh, my God, I used to know a girl who sang that.

NEIL

I have a cousin who still does.

CALLA

The girl I knew drowned herself.

87

NEIL

I wish my cousin had!

CALLA

You know, I've known a lot of girls who committed suicide.

JIMMY

Here, pass these.
(NEIL *takes two glasses from him*.)

NEIL

Miss Meldrum?

RHODA

Thanks. (*She takes it*.)

JIMMY

Calla?

CALLA

Thank you. (*She takes it*.)

NEIL
(*Going back for more*)
Does Daphne get any?

JIMMY

I don't know. Does she?

RHODA

Yes, of course she does.

88

NEIL

(*Handing* DAPHNE *a glass*)

Getting a big girl. When are we going to do another matinee, by the way?

DAPHNE

Whenever you say.

JIMMY

(*Raising his glass*)

Well, here's fun.

ALL

Fun! (*They drink.*)

JIMMY

Well, Rhoda, what about it? (*Points to the piano*) Shall *I* start? (*Reciting*) "Little Boy Blue," by Eugene Field:

"The little toy dog is covered with dust,
  Yet sturdy and staunch he stands . . ."

CALLA

Oh, I know that.

NEIL

So do I.

CALLA

"The little tin soldier is red with rust . . ."

NEIL

"And his musket moulds in his hands."

89

CALLA, NEIL, JIMMY and RHODA
(*Together in a loud crescendo*)
"Time was when the little toy dog was new
And the soldier was passing fair . . ."

JIMMY
"And that was the time when our Little Boy Blue"

NEIL
"Kissed them, and put them there."

JIMMY
Now, then—"Melisande in the Wood."

RHODA
Oh, very well. On your own heads be it. (*She crosses
to the piano.*)

JIMMY
(*In Cockney as she settles herself*)
She's got a lovely voice, me cousin Rhoda, when she
don't crack on the 'igh notes.

RHODA
(*Also in Cockney*)
You'd crack on the 'igh notes yourself, if you'd been
cleaning out the sink all day, like I 'ave, me boy. (*She
begins to play and sing the ballad "Melisande in the
Wood." The others gather around the piano, with their
champagne glasses. JIMMY interposes ribald comments*

90

from time to time, such as "Oh, look, she crossed her hands." On the phrase "All alone in the world" in the song, they all join in with burlesque intensity. When the song ends, RHODA *begins to strum some dance music.)*

JIMMY
(*To* CALLA)

Listen, that's "The Dollar Princess."

RHODA

Do you want to dance? (*She plays the waltz from "The Dollar Princess."* JIMMY *and* CALLA *dance together.* NEIL *stands leaning over the piano, looking at* RHODA. *In the middle of the dance,* MICHAEL's *voice is heard calling:*)

MICHAEL
(*Off*)

Jimmy! Jimmy! (MICHAEL *comes in, dressed in his shirt and trousers; shirt open and suspenders hanging.)*

JIMMY

Well, what's happened to you? Are you going to bed, or something?

MICHAEL

I bust the buttonhole in my other shirt. Mother said I was to ask you to put the studs in.

JIMMY

Oh, my God, can't you even do that for yourself? Come here.

91

MICHAEL

They screw in.

JIMMY

I know. Now stand still.

NEIL

(*To* RHODA)

Go on, won't you?

RHODA

(*Rising*)

That's quite enough.

DAPHNE

No, please, Rhoda, just one more.
(RHODA *shakes her head, and leaves the piano,
taking her glass with her.*)

JIMMY

Damn it, I've dropped it! (*Goes on his knees*) Where
is the doggone thing?
(DAPHNE *and* MICHAEL *join him on the floor.*)

NEIL

(*To* RHODA, *glancing at the group*)
I don't think we want to play this, do we?
(*Re-enter* MRS. RANDALL.)

MRS. RANDALL

Michael, what are you doing down here like that?

MICHAEL

Getting Jimmy to put my studs in. He dropped one of them.

MRS. RANDALL

Why in here of all places? Oh, good evening, Mr. Harding.

NEIL

Good evening, Mrs. Randall.

MRS. RANDALL
(*To* NEIL)

Excuse me a minute, will you? Jimmy, will you please hurry up with Michael? I want him to go out.

JIMMY
(*Still on his knees*)

Well, just as soon as I find this. . . . Calla, do you mind moving?

MICHAEL
(*Sitting up*)

Where do you want me to go?

MRS. RANDALL
(*To* RHODA)

The most infuriating thing has happened. Mazetti's haven't sent the Religieuse.

JIMMY
(*As before*)

The what?

MRS. RANDALL

The Religieuse. It's the dessert.

JIMMY

I always thought it was a nun!

MICHAEL

Oh, are we having one of those? Oh, goody. (*To* RHODA) It's ice cream, with little eclairs all around it.

JIMMY

Look, if you want me to put that stud in, you'd better help me find it.

RHODA

Let me help. (*She joins them.*)

MRS. RANDALL

I telephoned them, and they have it there all right, but there's no one in the Delivery to bring it. Apparently they have a big party on somewhere. So Michael will have to take a taxicab, and go for it.

JIMMY

Why can't they send it up by messenger?

MRS. RANDALL

And have it arrive all smashed to pieces? It has to be carried very carefully.

JIMMY

Well, considering the way Michael always drops things . . .

MICHAEL

You dropped the stud this time.

RHODA
(*Finding it*)

Here it is!

MRS. RANDALL

Oh, thank goodness. Now, then, Jimmy, please be quick. It really is too tiresome.

JIMMY

Now, hold still, for God's sake. Where did you get these damn-fool studs, anyway?

MICHAEL

They were Father's second-best ones.

JIMMY

Well, no wonder he never wore them. (*Fumbling*) Oh, damn the thing!

MRS. RANDALL

Really, Jimmy, if you can't manage a little thing like that . . .

JIMMY

All right, Mother, you come and try.

95

MRS. RANDALL

I shall do no such thing. But Michael's got to go. There's no one else to send. What is the time?

NEIL

It's twenty-five of ten, Mrs. Randall.

MRS. RANDALL

Oh, dear, they close at ten. What are we going to do? (*There is a slightly pointed pause.*)

NEIL

Would you like *me* to go for it, Mrs. Randall?

MRS. RANDALL
(*Insincerely*)

Oh, I wouldn't dream of such a thing.

NEIL
(*Equally so*)

I'd be glad to.

MRS. RANDALL

Well, it would be a kindness.

NEIL

Not at all.

MRS. RANDALL

Well, thank you so much, then. Daphne, go and telephone for a taxicab right away. And then call Mazetti's, and tell them there's someone coming right down.

NEIL

Why doesn't Daphne ride down with me, and keep me company?
(DAPHNE *pauses, arrested, at the door.*)

MRS. RANDALL

Daphne has to help me here.

RHODA

I'll do anything there is, Aunt Lucy.

NEIL

Won't you come too, and make a party of it?

RHODA

No, thank you.

DAPHNE

Can I go, Mother?

MRS. RANDALL

Well, it seems very silly to me, but if Mr. Harding wants company . . .

DAPHNE

I'll just get my coat. I shan't be a minute. (*She dashes off.*)

97

MRS. RANDALL
(*Calling after her*)

Call the cab first. (*To* NEIL) It's really very kind of you.

JIMMY
(*To* MICHAEL)

There's one done. Now, where's the other?

MRS. RANDALL
(*To* NEIL)

Daphne knows the address. You ring the night bell, and tell them it's for Mrs. Randall. You'll be careful, won't you? They're very fragile.

NEIL

I'll lift her up tenderly. (*He goes out.*)

JIMMY

You're incurable, Mother.

MRS. RANDALL

Mr. Harding offered.

JIMMY

After you'd made it impossible for him not to! You know it's snowing, don't you?

MRS. RANDALL

It isn't!

JIMMY

Started just as we came in.

MRS. RANDALL

Oh, dear, now what are we going to do? We should have had that marquee.

JIMMY

Mother, stop worrying. (*To* MICHAEL) There! Now I suppose you want me to tie your tie again?

MICHAEL

Oh, I left it upstairs. I'll get it.

MRS. RANDALL

Jimmy can come up to your room. And just a minute, Michael. Where did you go this afternoon?

MICHAEL

To the Hippodrome.

MRS. RANDALL

Are you sure?

MICHAEL

Yes. Why?

MRS. RANDALL

Then what's the program of *The Easiest Way* doing on your bureau? (*Glances exchanged around*) I'm very angry with you. You knew I didn't want you to see that.

99

MICHAEL

I don't see why not.

MRS. RANDALL

Never mind why not. I told you you weren't to go. And I don't like your telling me you'd been to the Hippodrome. Now, go on upstairs. I'll talk to you tomorrow.

MICHAEL
(*At the door*)

I heard you tell someone the play was a great lesson.

MRS. RANDALL

We won't argue it. Go along. (*He goes.*)

JIMMY

Mother, what's all the fuss about? You don't really think there was anything in the play he didn't know already, do you?

MRS. RANDALL

I certainly hope so.

JIMMY

Well, there's no harm in hoping.

MRS. RANDALL

And what did all those looks mean just now? Calla, did you know that was where he was going, when you gave him the money?

CALLA

I had an idea.

MRS. RANDALL

Well, then I'm very displeased with you. Did you know, Jimmy?

JIMMY

I knew he'd been. And I could have told you he'd go, the moment you forbade him.

MRS. RANDALL

And you, Rhoda?

RHODA

He told me he'd been.

MRS. RANDALL

Then why didn't you tell me?

RHODA

(*Protesting*)

Aunt Lucy, I'm not a sneak.

MRS. RANDALL

Rhoda, really! It's all very well for you and Jimmy to be friends with the children, but you needn't *conspire* with them. I'm extremely annoyed with you all. (*She goes into the dressing room.*)

CALLA

Well, that makes a pleasant start to the evening.

101

JIMMY

Oh, that'll soon blow over. She and Father went on just like that about me and *The Second Mrs. Tanqueray.*

CALLA

Yes, but this time it's not going to blow over quite so easily.

JIMMY

Why not?

CALLA

Because *I'm* involved in it. Jimmy, I think it's about time you realized that your mother doesn't like me. In case you haven't realized it, let me point it out to you. She hates me like poison.

(RHODA *rises.*)

JIMMY

Calla, what nonsense.

CALLA

It's true. (*She goes over for more champagne.*)

JIMMY

Of course it isn't true. Is it, Rhoda? Mother talks to you. She's very fond of Calla. (*Silence*) Isn't she?

CALLA

Go on. Deal with that one.

RHODA

Jimmy, I wouldn't go into this now.

CALLA

Why not?

RHODA

Because I don't think it's the time.

CALLA

Listen, I let you talk me into apologizing to her this afternoon, and I've been mad at myself ever since. So, Jimmy boy, with our engagement popping tonight, you might as well face it. *Your—mother—doesn't—like—me.* And Teacher's Pet, there, knows it perfectly well.

JIMMY

Calla!

CALLA

And all this fuss about *The Easiest Way* is because your mother thinks that's the story of my life!

JIMMY

Oh, don't be so silly!

CALLA

(*To* RHODA)

I bet she's told you that.

103

RHODA

(*Whose temper is fraying out quickly*)

No, she hasn't. But if she did think it, don't you think that might be a little bit your fault?

CALLA

What do you mean?

RHODA

Well, I don't know, but it seems to me that I've heard an awful lot since I've been here about—the temptations of the stage, and what a hard time you've had resisting them. . . .

CALLA

Are you insinuating . . . ?

RHODA

No, I'm not. But I just think you've talked a little too much about it—both of you, if you want to know—and if Aunt Lucy has got any such ideas, it's you who've put them there.

CALLA

It's easy enough for you to be smug. You've never known what it is to be up against it—not know where your next meal's coming from. . .

RHODA

(*Heatedly*)

I'm not being smug, and that's no argument.

JIMMY
(*Worried, but trying to be light about it*)
Now, girls!

CALLA
(*Over-riding him*)
Why isn't it any argument?

RHODA
(*Fiercely*)
I might just as well say that you've never known what
it is *not* to be up against it, and to know so damn well
where your next meal's coming from that you could
scream from the sheer boredom of life!

JIMMY
(*Shouting them down*)
What are you two talking about?

RHODA
(*Sitting again, rather huffily*)
I've no idea!

JIMMY
I don't know what's the matter with you both.
(*Enter* NORA *from the bedroom. She carries two
corsages.*)

NORA
Mr. Jimmy, the mistress says will you all please come
down? Judge Hazeltine's here, and there are some other
people just arriving.

JIMMY

Oh, all right, Nora. We'll be right down. (NORA *looks at the corsages, uncertain as to which belongs to whom.* JIMMY *takes them from her.*)

NORA

Thank you, Mr. Jimmy. Watch the pins. (*She goes out.* JIMMY *stands for a moment with the flowers, looking from* RHODA *to* CALLA *and back again.*)

JIMMY

Now, will you two please make it up? Remember, you've got to share a bedroom tonight!

RHODA

I'm sorry, Jimmy. Sorry, Calla.

CALLA

Oh, all right. I'm sorry, too.

JIMMY
(*Giving them their flowers*)

Well, that's all right, then. Let's go down. (*He holds the door open for them*) Oh, I've got to tie Michael's tie. You go ahead. I'll be right after you. (*The two girls go out.* JIMMY *stands for a moment in the doorway, thinking. Then he goes out.*)

CURTAIN

ACT TWO

Scene II

Scene: *The same. Later that night.*

When the curtain rises, Miss Pinner *is standing in the open doorway, listening to sounds coming from below. She has taken off her hat and is wearing a filmy scarf, by way of dressing for the occasion. She has a glass of champagne in her hand. On the end-table, placed in front of the center chair, is a supper tray, with a pint bottle of champagne.* Nora *stands hovering between the open door and the dressing-room doors, which are also open. From below comes the sound of a number of voices singing "For They Are Jolly Good Fellows."*

MISS PINNER

Oh, listen to that. It always makes me cry. (*The final hurrahs come up*) Did you drink their healths, Nora?

NORA

Me?

MISS PINNER

Oh, you must drink their healths. Is there another glass? Well, never mind, take mine. (*She comes back to the table, partly refills the glass*) There!
(NORA *drinks, rather foolishly.*)

NORA

So he's really going through with it.

MISS PINNER

Why, Nora, whatever do you mean?

NORA

There won't be any getting out of it, after that.

MISS PINNER

But, Nora, why should anyone want to get out of it?

NORA

The mistress thought he would. Well, I'd better be getting back in there, before they all come trooping up from supper. Are you through with your tray?

MISS PINNER

Oh, yes. Yes, thanks. (NORA *takes it*) Nora, has Mrs. Randall talked to you?

NORA

Sure, she's talked to me. She's talked to you, too, hasn't she?

MISS PINNER

She's said a few things.

NORA

Sure. She's talked to everyone. Except Mr. Jimmy. (*She goes out with the tray into the dressing room.* MISS PINNER *consults the watch pinned to her dress.*)

MISS PINNER

Half-past twelve! Mercy!
(*Enter* MRS. RANDALL.)

MRS. RANDALL

Oh, you're still here, Miss Jessie. Did you hear the speeches?

MISS PINNER

Yes, they were very clever.

MRS. RANDALL

Well, there's no turning back now.

MISS PINNER

You mustn't be unhappy, Mrs. Randall. . . .

MRS. RANDALL

Well, it's no good talking about it. And no one but you knows what I really feel, that's one comfort.

MISS PINNER

(*Too brightly, because this remark makes her vaguely uncomfortable*)

The dance is going beautifully, isn't it? I took a peek just before supper—you know, through the open door—and it looked so pretty. All the brightly colored dresses, and the lights. I saw Miss Meldrum waltzing with Mr. Harding. Is she having a good time?

MRS. RANDALL

I hope so. He's being very attentive to her. Almost too attentive. I thought they were a little conspicuous.

MISS PINNER

You don't think that could *be* anything, do you?

MRS. RANDALL

Do you mean a romance? (*With a light laugh*) Oh, Miss Jessie, no. You know what a ladies' man he's always been. A nice, quiet girl like Rhoda would be the last kind he'd be interested in.

MISS PINNER

Even ladies' men settle down, and get married one day. And Miss Meldrum has money, you said.

MRS. RANDALL

You know as well as I do, the Hardings don't need money. No, Jimmy must have told Neil. . . .

(*Enter* JIMMY.)

MISS PINNER

Oh, here is Jimmy. I hoped I'd get a peek at you.

JIMMY

Surely, these are very late hours for you, Miss Jessie?

MISS PINNER

I had to stay up and drink your health. May I congratulate you?

JIMMY

Thank you.

MISS PINNER

I hope you'll be very happy.

JIMMY

I'm quite sure I shall.

MISS PINNER

Well, now I really must be getting home.

MRS. RANDALL

Michael will take you.

MISS PINNER

Oh, that isn't in the least necessary. If he can just call me a cab . . .

MRS. RANDALL

No, he'll take you. He knows he's got to.

III

MISS PINNER

Well, it's always nice to be taken home by a gentleman. Good night, Mrs. Randall, dear, and thank you again so much.

MRS. RANDALL

Good night, Miss Jessie.

MISS PINNER
(*To* JIMMY)

Now the next thing will be the wedding. Good night.

JIMMY

Good night, Miss Jessie. (*She goes*) Well, Mother, satisfied with everything?

MRS. RANDALL

Yes, dear, I think so.

JIMMY

You're not—unhappy about it, are you?

MRS. RANDALL

Unhappy? No, of course not.

JIMMY

You were crying downstairs.

MRS. RANDALL

Well, it's a little bit of a wrench, but . . . I only want

you to be happy, Jimmy. (*She goes to him*) I hope you will be. Very. (*She kisses him.* CALLA *comes in from the dressing room. Girls' voices are heard, off, when the door opens*) And you, too, Calla.

CALLA

Me, too, what?

MRS. RANDALL

I was just wishing Jimmy happiness.

CALLA

Oh.

MRS. RANDALL

I hope you'll both be very happy. Come and kiss me. (CALLA *comes to her. The kiss is performed.* MRS. RANDALL *dabs at her eyes*) I'm glad we've had this minute alone. Did you think the supper was all right?

JIMMY

Sure.

MRS. RANDALL

I thought Mr. Harding's speech was a little—facetious.

JIMMY

Well, it was brief, which was the main thing.

MRS. RANDALL

I think you should have said a little more than you did.

113

JIMMY

Mother, if you want to know, I find the whole of to-night's proceedings a little grisly, and my one idea is to get them over as quickly as possible.

MRS. RANDALL

Jimmy, that's not very kind. When I've gone to all this trouble.

JIMMY

I'm sorry. I was kidding.

MRS. RANDALL
(*Smiling wanly*)

Well, I'll just go and see that everything's all right in here. (*She goes into dressing room. Female voices heard, off, again.* JIMMY *takes out his cigarette case.*)

CALLA

Do you suppose I could have one of those? (*He gives her one and lights it.*)

JIMMY
(*Looking round for an ash-tray*)

Oh, damn, I forgot again. (*He returns to the waste-basket.*)

CALLA

Were you kidding? Or is this party really your idea of hell, the way it is mine?

JIMMY

Calla, I've had this sort of thing ever since I can remember.

CALLA

I don't see what that's got to do with it. Who are all these people, anyway?

JIMMY

Friends of ours.

CALLA

Yours?

JIMMY

Some of them.

CALLA

The gink with a face like a kneecap, who thinks it's cute to squeeze you when you dance? He's almost as bad as the Judge. I guess it's because I'm an actress. You can take liberties with actresses.

JIMMY
(*Lightly*)

Who was that?

CALLA

I don't know. Stebbings, or some such name.

JIMMY

Oh, Chuck Stebbings.

CALLA

Who's he?

JIMMY

He married Betty Henderson.

CALLA

And who's Betty Henderson?

JIMMY

She's wearing blue—with a feather-brush thing in her hair. A—vinaigrette, or whatever you call it. Betty used to be considered fast. She got herself into quite a scandal a few years back.

CALLA

Oh—how?

JIMMY

She met a man at a dance, and next day she was seen lunching with him at Claremont. She got into awful hot water. People stopped asking her out. . . .

CALLA

My God—just for a lunch?

JIMMY

Oh, she had a hell of a time till Chuck married her, and that was considered pretty brave of him. Mother and her mother were at school together.

CALLA

And do you like her—or her brave, pinching husband?

JIMMY

Not particularly.

CALLA

Do we have to know people like that after we're married? Because your mothers went to school together?

JIMMY

Know them—yes.

CALLA

See them?

JIMMY

Now and then.

CALLA

Why, if you don't like them?

JIMMY

Because they're people that I've always known. We can't just drop them.

CALLA

Why don't we make a bargain? One night a week, your friends—if you call them friends—people like that— and family. . . .

JIMMY

And the rest of the week?

CALLA

We have fun.

JIMMY

Well, we'll see.

CALLA

You know, there's a lot I can't make out about you. You don't really enjoy a party like tonight's. . . . You do enjoy the kind of party that—well, the kind of party that we met at. But you still cling to all this.

JIMMY

It's my background.

CALLA

You like to escape from it, but you always want to come back, is that it?

JIMMY

Maybe.

CALLA

And what sort of a prospect is that for me?

JIMMY

Well, doesn't it work both ways? You were sick of your kind of life—you said.

CALLA

I know I did.

JIMMY

Wasn't it true?

CALLA

I guess. In a way.

JIMMY

Well, then . . .

CALLA

Okay, for the present.

JIMMY

That sounds like a threat.

CALLA

No more than your "We'll see."

JIMMY

Oh, Calla, don't let's quarrel.

CALLA

I'm not quarreling.

JIMMY

Good. It'll work out all right. You'll see. (*Takes her hand*) Kiss me?

CALLA

Sure. (*They kiss.* RHODA *comes in.*)

RHODA

Oh, I beg your pardon.

JIMMY

It's all right. We're engaged. Come on in, the water's fine. How about a drink?

RHODA

The band will be starting again any minute.

JIMMY

A quick one.

CALLA

Rhoda, are you through in your room? I think I'll go up. There was such a crush in there.

RHODA

Of course.

CALLA

Won't be a minute. (*She goes out.*)

JIMMY

Are you having a good time?

RHODA

Yes, thanks.

JIMMY

Here. (*He gives her a glass, and takes one for himself*) Well . . .

RHODA

Congratulations, Jimmy. I hope you'll be very happy.

JIMMY
(*Soberly*)

Thanks. (*She drinks. Then he does*) Rhoda, what was all that about earlier this evening?

RHODA
(*Evasively*)

Oh—nothing, I think.

JIMMY

Is it true that Mother doesn't like Calla?

RHODA

I don't think she understands her.

JIMMY
(*Reflectively*)

No.

RHODA

But that doesn't matter, does it? *You* like her. You want to marry her. That's all that matters, surely?

JIMMY

I guess so. But all the rest—what you said about her past life—what was that about?

RHODA

Nothing. I shouldn't have said it. It was quite unforgivable. I'm very sorry, Jimmy.

JIMMY

I don't think you quite understand. After all, there is something in what Calla says. You've been brought up so differently. You've never known that world.

RHODA

No, I know.

JIMMY

Besides, Calla's very attractive. To men. Even before she went on the stage—when she was quite a kid—she always had men after her.

RHODA

Yes, of course she did.

JIMMY

Women like Mother don't understand that. I don't think you do, either. I mean, to anyone who's not always had that sort of thing, anyone who has, seems— oh, I don't know—*suspect*. It's not a girl's fault if she's attractive.

RHODA

Fault?

JIMMY
(*Angrily*)

It's very easy to condemn if you've never had any temptations.

(RHODA's *mouth opens in amazement.* MRS. RANDALL *returns. Voices as before.*)

MRS. RANDALL

Jimmy, are you still up here? You must go down.

JIMMY

All right, I'm going. Coming, Rhoda?

MRS. RANDALL

I want to speak to Rhoda just a minute.

JIMMY

Oh, all right, then. (*He goes.* MRS. RANDALL *seizes his empty glass and replaces it on the drink-table.*)

RHODA

Did you want me, Aunt Lucy?

MRS. RANDALL

Just for a moment. Are you all right? Have you plenty of partners?

RHODA

Yes, thank you.

MRS. RANDALL

Have you danced with the Judge yet?

RHODA

Twice.

MRS. RANDALL

That's nice. You know, he's very fond of dancing.

RHODA

Yes, he seems to be.

MRS. RANDALL

Whom do you have the next one with?

RHODA

(*Looking at her program*)

Mr. Harding.

MRS. RANDALL

You don't think you're dancing with him too often, do you?

RHODA

I hope not.

MRS. RANDALL

How many did he take?

RHODA

I forget exactly. Four or five.

MRS. RANDALL

Well, that's quite enough. Not that I don't want you to have a good time. But you have to remember you're a stranger here, and people are apt to notice everything you do.

RHODA

(*With control*)

Of course, Aunt Lucy.

MRS. RANDALL

It's one thing for Mr. Harding to be attentive. I expect Jimmy told him to be. But men don't always realize . . .

RHODA
(*With great control*)

No, Aunt Lucy.

MRS. RANDALL
(*With a smile*)

That's all, dear. (*She picks up* RHODA's *glass to re-place it.*)

RHODA
(*Firmly*)

I haven't finished with that.
(*Their eyes meet for a moment. Then* MRS. RAN-
DALL *drops hers.*)

MRS. RANDALL
(*Defeated momentarily*)

Oh . . . (DAPHNE *comes in*) Has the band finished supper?

DAPHNE

I think they're smoking.

MRS. RANDALL

They must get started again, right away. I don't want this to go on beyond two o'clock. (*She goes out.*)

DAPHNE

Well, what do you think of him?

RHODA

Whom?

DAPHNE

Neil. I saw you dancing with him.

RHODA

Oh, yes. Well, I agree he's attractive. But—I think he knows he is.

DAPHNE

He thinks *you* are. He talked a lot about you in the taxi this evening.

RHODA

I'm sorry.

DAPHNE

Why?

RHODA

Well, that wasn't exactly what you wanted, was it? To talk about me?

DAPHNE

I was glad to have that. I think he was sore at being made to go, and just asked me so as not to have to go alone.

RHODA

Did you enjoy it?

DAPHNE

I enjoyed being with him. Nothing happened, of course. I never thought it would, but all the time I was wondering—if it did—what I ought to do about it. Mother told me once that no self-respecting girl lets herself be kissed by a man she isn't engaged to. Is that true?

RHODA
(*Stalling*)

Yes. In a way.

DAPHNE

Haven't *you* been kissed?

RHODA

Not very often. Once or twice.

DAPHNE

Well, then, it isn't wrong?

RHODA

Wrong—no. But you want to be—well, you don't want
to be—well, it depends.

DAPHNE

You mean, you don't want to let *everyone* kiss you?

RHODA

Yes, exactly.
(*Music starts below.*)

DAPHNE

He wanted to know a lot about you.

RHODA
(*With a smile*)

And what did you tell him?

DAPHNE

Oh, I told him about you. I told him you said you weren't attractive to men.

RHODA

Daphne! You didn't!

DAPHNE

He said you were joshing me. I told him you were serious.

RHODA

Daphne!

DAPHNE

He thinks you're mysterious.

RHODA

What on earth made you tell him that?

DAPHNE

(*Faltering slightly*)

Well, you said so. . . .

RHODA

I might have said I had a spot on my back, or that my hair wasn't my own, but you don't have to tell other people that. Really!

DAPHNE

(*Rather ashamed of herself*)

No, I guess it was silly of me. It was just that . . .

well, talking to him, I didn't think. But I am sorry. I know it was silly of me now.

RHODA

(*Repentant before* DAPHNE's *evident distress*)

Oh, it's all right, really. It doesn't matter. Listen, the music's started. Aren't you dancing this one?

DAPHNE

Yes. Are you?

RHODA

I think I'm going to cut it.

DAPHNE

Why?

RHODA

I've got a bit of a headache. It's the noise and the hot rooms.

DAPHNE

Oh, that's too bad. Would you like a headache powder?

RHODA

I took one right after supper. I think I'll just stay up here for a few minutes and give it a chance to work. You run along.

DAPHNE

Would you like some of these lights out?

RHODA

Yes. All right. Some of them.

DAPHNE
(*Switching off the wall-brackets*)
How's that?

RHODA

That's very nice.

DAPHNE

Well . . . (*She opens the door. The music is heard louder from below.* DAPHNE *pauses*) I'm sorry, Rhoda.

RHODA

It's all right. (DAPHNE *goes.* RHODA, *near the end of her tether with depression, nerves and irritation, remains slumped in her chair. She finishes her glass of champagne, looks around and then, with a certain decision, goes over and pours herself another. She sips at it, then sets it down, crosses to the window where she draws the curtains and stands looking out.* NEIL *comes in. She has her back to him.*)

NEIL

Miss Meldrum, I believe.

RHODA
(*Turning*)
Oh—hello.

NEIL

What were you looking at? Has there been an accident?

RHODA

No, I was looking at the snow. It's quite thick already.

NEIL

Have you never seen New York under snow?

RHODA

No, I've seen pictures of it.

NEIL

It really is quite beautiful. Especially in Central Park. You should drive around it—at night. Central Park under snow in a hansom at night is one of my hobbies.

RHODA

(*Casually, not to be drawn*)

It sounds lovely.

NEIL

It is. Well, I think this is our dance.

RHODA

Oh, yes, it is.

NEIL

Shall we go down? Or would you rather sit it out up here?

RHODA

Would you mind?

NEIL

I'd like it. How about having some of that—good champagne?

RHODA

I . . . er . . . I have some.

NEIL

Oh, a solitary drinker?

RHODA

Well . . . on this occasion.

NEIL

Would it spoil your fun if I joined you?

RHODA

Please do.

NEIL

(*Helping himself*)

Is that to—help you through the evening? Are you being very bored?

RHODA

No. What makes you think that?

NEIL

Well, you've been looking it—a little.

RHODA

I have?

NEIL

Oh, in the nicest, and politest, and most English way possible.

RHODA

I had a headache.

NEIL

Oh, come now.

RHODA

What do you mean?

NEIL

People don't have headaches. Nobody has headaches.

RHODA

You try dancing with Judge Hazeltine! No, I shouldn't have said that.

NEIL

Why not?

RHODA

Oh, because he's very kind. . . .

NEIL

Is that the word?

RHODA

What do you mean?

NEIL

Well, Judge Hazeltine has quite a reputation.

RHODA

You mean, as a . . . ?

NEIL

Exactly.

RHODA

Really?

NEIL

Oh, yes. He's quite well known for it. To everyone except Mrs. Randall, I think. Didn't you notice anything?

RHODA

I thought it was—accidental—or else my imagination.

NEIL

No, there was nothing accidental or imaginary about it. Still, after that, we'll allow you the headache. Would a cigarette help it?

RHODA

Yes, I think it might. (*He gives her one, lights it for her and then looks around for an ash-tray. Laconically*) There isn't one.

NEIL

Oh, no, I remember.

(*With sudden decision* RHODA *reaches out her hand to the candy-dish, tipping its contents onto the table, and hands him the empty dish with a gesture of defiance.*)

134

RHODA

Here.

NEIL

(*Amused*)

Thank you—very much. (*He settles himself*) Tell me about girls who've been presented at Court.

RHODA

What do you want to know?

NEIL

I've never known any and I'm scared of the idea of them. I'm a little scared of *you*.

RHODA

(*Reacting slightly to the champagne and the atmosphere of flirtation*)

What are you scared of?

NEIL

I don't know what you're thinking. I know you're thinking something, and I don't know what it is.

RHODA

You don't know what I'm thinking about what?

NEIL

Anything. The dance—America—me . . .

135

RHODA

I'm enjoying them all a great deal.

NEIL

Well, that's encouraging if you mean it. But, you see, I don't know if you mean it. I've danced with you three times. . . . We've talked about nothing. . . . I heard you sing in here this evening—but I don't know whether any of that is really you. I don't think it is. I think somewhere deep down, you're quite, quite different.

RHODA

(*Flicking her ash on the carpet*)
What do you think I am—deep down?

NEIL

I don't know. And that's what fascinates me. You know, I've never met anyone about whom I've heard more conflicting reports than I have about you.

RHODA

Oh, really? Who from?

NEIL

Jimmy—Daphne—Michael. They all seem to see you quite differently. Which of them's right? If any?

RHODA

I don't know what they've said.

136

NEIL

Shall I tell you?

RHODA
(*Shying*)

No, I don't think so.

NEIL

Michael has an idea you're—fast.

RHODA

Did he say that?

NEIL

He implied it.

RHODA

Michael needs smacking.

NEIL

He meant it very complimentarily. Why did you tell Daphne you weren't attractive to men?

RHODA

I . . . I . . .

NEIL

Well?

RHODA

I can't think of an answer for that, that wouldn't sound like—fishing.

NEIL

You know it isn't true.

137

RHODA

Do I?

NEIL

You've got a kind of—light inside you. It's only just beginning to come on. I've known all evening it was there, if only one could find the switch. You're quite different now it's on. Has anyone ever told you that you look like the Sphinx?

RHODA

No, but I've seen the Sphinx, and it isn't really a compliment.

NEIL

No?

RHODA

No, it's very battered with a broken nose.

NEIL

Oh, I'm sorry. But you see, I haven't seen it. Isn't it—mysterious and inscrutable, the way it's written up?

RHODA

I think it's more—the idea of it.

NEIL

Well, that's what I meant about you. I think you could be dangerous, too. If you weren't being English, and would let yourself. You know, we're in America.

(*His hand touches hers for a moment and she withdraws it.*)

RHODA
(*In an odd voice*)
What did Jimmy say about me?

NEIL
Jimmy's a fool. He doesn't know anything about women.
  (*There is a pause. Disturbed, she rises and moves away from him, walking to the window.*)

RHODA
It's still snowing.

NEIL
  (*Coming close behind her to look*)
It's still beautiful.

RHODA
(*More because she is at a loss for what to say, than for any other reason*)
There's a poem about London snow . . .

NEIL
(*Very quietly*)
What is it?

RHODA
(*Quoting*)
"When men were all asleep, the snow came flying,
 In large white flakes upon the city brown,

Stealthily and perpetually settling and loosely lying,
Hushing the latest traffic of the drowsy town . . ."

NEIL

I like that. (*She turns away from the window. They
face each other and he kisses her. They hold the kiss for
a moment; then, as they separate, he catches her hands*)
Let's go out and look at it.

RHODA

We can't.

NEIL

Why not? Come out and look at Central Park in
the snow.

RHODA

We can't leave the dance.

NEIL

We can, if we want to. And I want to. Don't you?

RHODA

We can't.

NEIL

It won't take more than half an hour. No one will
notice.

RHODA

Yes, they will.

140

Neil

Then let them. What do you care? Listen, down there, there's a bad band playing bad music, and a lot of people dancing very badly on a crowded, bad floor. They're people you've never seen in your life before, and will probably never see again. Out there is something else that you may never see again. New York in the snow. Please let me show it to you.

Rhoda

But how can we?

Neil

Just get a coat and something to put over your head. If anyone sees you, you can say you're going to get a breath of air for your headache. I'll slip out first. I'll meet you at the corner. We'll drive down to the Plaza, and then get a hansom. Won't you? Won't you?

Rhoda

I shouldn't.

Neil

But you will?

Rhoda

All right. For just half an hour.

Neil

Good. I'll go down first. You will come?

RHODA
(*Gaily*)

Yes.

(*He smiles at her and goes out, leaving the door open. The music swells up from below. RHODA stands for a moment, and then moves happily across the room. She stops halfway for an instant to look back at the window, her face radiant, and then starts quickly for the door.*)

CURTAIN

ACT THREE

ACT THREE

Scene I

Scene: *The Same. Around noon. The next day.*

When the curtain rises, Mrs. Randall *is discovered writing letters.* Miss Pinner *appears at the door.*

Miss Pinner
May I come in?

Mrs. Randall
Oh, Miss Jessie. (*Rises*) Yes, of course, come in. Take off your coat, so you won't catch cold, when you go out.

Miss Pinner
(*Doing so*)
I thought you'd probably all sleep late—but I have appointments all the afternoon, and you did say . . .

Mrs. Randall
Of course. I told Nellie to put the stuff up for you. There was quite a lot of the mousse of ham left.

Miss Pinner
Mother's very excited. Did you get a good night's rest?

MRS. RANDALL

I didn't close an eye.

MISS PINNER

Oh, dear . . . There wasn't anything the matter, was
there?

MRS. RANDALL

Yes, I was terribly upset.

MISS PINNER

Oh, Mrs. Randall, dear. What—what has Miss Longstreth done now?

MRS. RANDALL

It wasn't Calla this time—for a wonder. It was Rhoda.
I don't understand it. I just don't understand it!

MISS PINNER

But, Mrs. Randall, dear—what?

MRS. RANDALL

You won't believe it, Miss Jessie. You just won't believe it, but last night at the dance, what should she do
but disappear for nearly two hours with Neil Harding?

MISS PINNER

Disappear?

MRS. RANDALL

Completely. They went for a drive in the park, if you please.

MISS PINNER

Alone?

MRS. RANDALL

Quite alone.

MISS PINNER

Was their absence remarked?

MRS. RANDALL

Naturally. Two people can't just disappear like that without everyone knowing. I couldn't believe it at first. I looked everywhere. I thought she must have got locked in some place.

MISS PINNER

Did you speak to her when she returned?

MRS. RANDALL

I couldn't get her alone. Mr. Harding stayed on and on. She went to bed before he left, and Calla was sharing her room, so I couldn't say anything. I just lay awake all night with it. And this morning, she's gone out. Apparently she went out for a walk at eight o'clock. Jimmy's out, too. He went for a walk, as well.

MISS PINNER

With her?

MRS. RANDALL

No, Nora says they went separately. Everyone else is still asleep. I've been sitting here all by myself since nine with no one to talk to. Do you wonder I'm upset?

(*Enter* NORA *with a large florist's box.*)

NORA

These just came for you, madam.

MRS. RANDALL

Oh, thank you, Nora.

NORA

And your package is all ready, Miss Jessie. It's on the hall table.

MISS PINNER

Oh, thank you. (NORA *goes*) Flowers!

MRS. RANDALL

(*Going to the desk for scissors*)

The Judge called me up quite early. He was very concerned about it. And Julia Henderson. Apparently Neil cut a dance with Betty, and she called her mother the first thing to talk about it all and tell her what had happened.

MISS PINNER

Oh, but that's dreadful.

MRS. RANDALL

It'll be all over New York by lunchtime. (*She comes back and opens the flowers. Takes out card*) Neil Harding!

MISS PINNER
(*At a loss for how to take this*)
Oh. Oh. (*Then, rallying*) They're very lovely!

MRS. RANDALL

Conscience money! It's all very well for him. *She* hasn't sent me flowers, you notice. (*Enter* RHODA. *She wears winter walking dress and furs*) Oh, there you are. Where have you been?

RHODA

I've been for a walk. Oh, good morning, Miss Jessie.

MISS PINNER

Good morning, Miss Meldrum. (*Aware of atmosphere*) Well, I must be making tracks. Good-bye, Mrs. Randall, dear, and if there's anything I can *do* . . .

MRS. RANDALL

Thank you, Miss Jessie. But just—don't talk about it, or discuss it.

MISS PINNER

Oh, as if I would! (*With a world of reproof in her voice*) Good-bye, Miss Meldrum.

RHODA

Good-bye. (MISS PINNER *goes*) Well, I'll go and take off my things.

MRS. RANDALL

Rhoda, I want to talk to you.

RHODA

(*Returning*)

I know, Aunt Lucy. I'm sorry about last night.

MRS. RANDALL

Sorry!

RHODA

There's nothing I can say.

MRS. RANDALL

I'm glad you realize it. (*Bursting out*) What possessed you? Rhoda, what possessed you?

RHODA

I don't know.

MRS. RANDALL

To go off like that . . .

RHODA

I know.

MRS. RANDALL

You, of all people! If it had been Calla, I could

have understood it—but *you,* who've been properly brought up! . . .

RHODA

I know.

MRS. RANDALL

It's unheard of! Simply unheard of!

RHODA

Yes, I know.

MRS. RANDALL

Well, you might say something, instead of just "I know. I know" like that! Where did you go—exactly?

RHODA

I told you. Round the park.

MRS. RANDALL

Did he make love to you?

RHODA

Aunt Lucy, that is a question I have no intention of answering.

MRS. RANDALL

That means he did.

RHODA

I don't see why you think that. It might equally well mean that he didn't.

MRS. RANDALL

Well, that's beside the point. Which is, what am I going to do with you?

RHODA

Do with me?

MRS. RANDALL

Yes, do with you. You must realize what this means, and that you'll be thoroughly compromised.

RHODA

I know. (*Catching herself*) I'm sorry, Aunt Lucy. But I do know.

MRS. RANDALL

Everyone is talking about it. Everyone. Didn't you think of that, before you went?

RHODA

Not very much.

MRS. RANDALL

What made you? What made you?

RHODA

I wanted to. That isn't any excuse, I know. But I wanted to.

MRS. RANDALL

I can't think what your mother will say when she hears. I've had to write and tell her.

RHODA

What—already?

MRS. RANDALL

I've had to explain why I can't do anything about you. Because I can't, you know. Any chances you may have had are completely ruined. I should have thought, if you had nothing else to restrain you, that at least might have occurred to you.

RHODA

It never occurred to me I had any chances to ruin.

MRS. RANDALL

Well, that's what you came over here for, wasn't it?

RHODA
(*Indignantly*)

No!

MRS. RANDALL

Well, why did you come?

RHODA

I came because I wanted to.

MRS. RANDALL

That seems to be the only reason you can give for anything.

RHODA

It seems to me a good one.

153

MRS. RANDALL

If you think you can go through life doing everything you want to . . .

RHODA

I don't. I've spent almost my entire life not doing *anything* I wanted to. Or not being able to.

MRS. RANDALL

Well, I wash my hands of you, from now on. I don't know what you're going to do. You'd better go and stay with your Aunt Bessie in Indianapolis, if she'll have you, till it's blown over. If it ever does blow over. I've just been writing to her.

RHODA
(*Mockingly*)
Do you think I'd have any—chances in Indianapolis?

MRS. RANDALL

Rhoda, what's come over you? You never used to be flippant and defiant like this. I always thought you were such a nice girl.

RHODA

So did I, Aunt Lucy. It seems we were both wrong.

MRS. RANDALL

If that's how you're going to talk, I've no more to say to you. (*She takes up the flowers*) I'm going to put these in water, and then I shall get everyone up. You

154

know we're lunching out to save the servants. If you prefer to have yours on a tray, I daresay Nellie can manage something. (*She goes.* RHODA *takes off her hat, and makes as if to leave.* JIMMY *comes in.*)

RHODA

Hello. Why aren't you at the office?

JIMMY

I'm taking the morning off. Maybe the day. Where are you going?

RHODA

To take my things upstairs.

JIMMY

Give them to me. I want to talk to you.

RHODA

You, too?

JIMMY

What do you mean?

RHODA

Well, Aunt Lucy's just been talking to me.

JIMMY

What about?

RHODA

About last night.

155

JIMMY
(*Laying aside her things*)

What happened last night?

RHODA

Do you mean to say you don't know?

JIMMY

Oh, you mean you and Neil going off for a drive? Yes,
I was afraid Mother was going to blow off about that.
Although I thought perhaps as it was you . . .

RHODA

That seems to have made it worse.

JIMMY

Well, it's a lot of nonsense. Oh, I suppose it didn't
look very good—leaving the party—though God knows
it was grim enough. Was Mother very mad?

RHODA

I'm being sent to Indianapolis.

JIMMY

Why, is there a Federal Penitentiary there, or something?

RHODA

No, there's Aunt Bessie. What's she like, by the way?

JIMMY
(*With meaning*)
You won't have a very good time.

RHODA
I think that's the idea.

JIMMY
Do you mean you're in disgrace?

RHODA
Exactly.

JIMMY
You don't mean Mother thinks . . .

RHODA
What?

JIMMY
Well, that she thinks you're compromised, or something?

RHODA
Yes.

JIMMY
Oh, it's lunatic.

RHODA
It's not. She's quite right. It was an idiotic thing for me to have done, and I must have been quite mad.

157

JIMMY

You mean—you really think you've—blotted your copybook?

RHODA

Yes, I know I have.

JIMMY

Oh, it's ridiculous. You're all behaving as if he'd seduced you.

RHODA

The conventions of Society are that if a man and woman are in a position where he *could* have seduced her, it doesn't make any difference whether he did or not.

JIMMY
(*Struck*)

I never thought of it like that.

RHODA

Well, it's true. It's the basis on which every girl is brought up.

JIMMY

How damn silly!

RHODA

It's not really. It's just taking the worst view of human nature. And I've been a fool, that's all.

JIMMY

This will all blow over.

RHODA

That's what you think about everything.

JIMMY

Well, everything does, doesn't it? (*With a change of voice*) Almost everything. (*The serious note in his voice catches her attention. She looks at him.*)

RHODA

What do you mean by that?

JIMMY

Rhoda, I'm the one who's been a fool.

RHODA

How?

JIMMY

Calla.

RHODA

I don't understand.

JIMMY

I don't want to marry her. There, now I've said it. At last I've said it—out loud and to someone else. I've been saying it to myself all morning. I've been spending the last three months trying not to say it to myself.

RHODA

You mean—from the beginning . . . ?

159

JIMMY

Almost from the beginning. Only I wouldn't face it. I think it was only here last night when she said Mother didn't like her that I faced it properly.

RHODA

But—why should that have made a difference?

JIMMY

Oh, it wasn't that it was Mother. It could have been anybody. But haven't you ever noticed how you can go on saying that you like something—kidding yourself you like it—and then someone comes along and says they *don't* like it, and quite suddenly you know that you don't either, and that you've always known you didn't?

RHODA

Yes—with a book or a play or something to eat . . .

JIMMY

Well, it was just like that with Calla. And I had to wait till last night before I was able to admit it. A couple of hours before our engagement was announced. You can imagine how I felt. I'm afraid I took it out on you.

RHODA

That's all right.

JIMMY

(*Patting her shoulder*)

Good old Rhoda. You're always there, aren't you?

RHODA

(*After a moment*)

What are you going to do?

JIMMY

Nothing. What can I do?

RHODA

An engagement isn't a marriage.

JIMMY

I can't let her down. I've promised her marriage. Security, and permanence. They're things she's never had. She's been up against it all her life. (*Hastily*) Oh, I don't only mean the way we talked about last night. Though that, too. And then, there again. . . .

RHODA

What—there again?

JIMMY

Well, that's another reason why I can't do anything.

RHODA

Do you mean that—you and she . . . ? (JIMMY *nods*) Oh, I see. (*She seems to retreat into herself somewhat.*)

JIMMY

So there you are.

RHODA

Then all this talk about her being a good girl . . .

JIMMY

She was.

RHODA

She's not going to have a baby?

JIMMY
(*With a laugh*)

No! I almost wish she were, in a way. But it just makes it more impossible, that's all. Oh, it's no good talking about it. But I just wanted to say it once—to someone. And I always have confided in you.

RHODA

You mean, you're really going to marry her, feeling like that?

JIMMY

I can't do anything else. Oh, don't look so tragic. I daresay it won't be any worse than most marriages. Only it seems so silly to have waited until my age for this. If I'd been nineteen, there might have been some excuse. I guess I've just never grown up, or I'd have learned about . . . tinsel before now. (*He gives her a sad, rueful little smile*) It is silly, isn't it?

RHODA

I wish I could do something to help you.
   (*Enter* CALLA. *She wears a wrapper, and looks rather tousled.*)

JIMMY

Oh, hello, you're up?

CALLA

I came down for a cigarette.

JIMMY
(*Giving her one*)

Here.

CALLA

Thanks.

JIMMY
(*Kissing her*)

How are you?

CALLA

I'm fine.

JIMMY

What time do you want to lunch?

CALLA

Oh—about an hour?
   (MRS. RANDALL *returns carrying* NEIL'S *flowers in a vase.*)

163

MRS. RANDALL

Oh, good morning, Calla.

CALLA
(*Concealing the unlighted cigarette*)

Good morning, Mrs. Randall.

JIMMY
(*Indicating the flowers*)

Where did those come from?

MRS. RANDALL

Neil Harding sent them. (*There is a moment's significant silence.*)

JIMMY

Oh . . . Well, that was nice of him, wasn't it? I think I'll go and shave. I was out early. (*He goes out, quickly.*)

MRS. RANDALL

Calla, you really shouldn't go wandering around the house in your wrapper like that!

CALLA
(*Wearily*)

I'm sorry.

MRS. RANDALL

And there's something I want to ask you. Did you know that you promised two dances to the Judge last night, and then danced them both with someone else? (RHODA *rises to leave*) Where are you going, Rhoda?

RHODA

To take my things upstairs.

MRS. RANDALL

You'd better leave them here. We shall be going out quite soon.

RHODA

I thought you said . . .

MRS. RANDALL

I've changed my mind. Nellie isn't feeling well. I didn't like to ask her. You'll have to come to lunch with us. (*Returning to* CALLA) Well, Calla?

CALLA

Yes, I know I did.

MRS. RANDALL

Why did you?

CALLA

Because I don't like dancing with him.

MRS. RANDALL

Why not?

CALLA

Well, if you want to know—because he pinches!

MRS. RANDALL

What on earth do you mean?

CALLA

I mean he pinches. I'm sorry, Mrs. Randall, but Judge Hazeltine is a nasty old man!

MRS. RANDALL

Calla!

CALLA

He's been trying to paw me ever since he first met me.

MRS. RANDALL

Calla, that is a deliberate and disgusting lie!

CALLA

I know his type well.

MRS. RANDALL

Judge Hazeltine is one of the most respected men in New York.

CALLA

Yes, they always are!

RHODA

I'm afraid Calla is right, Aunt Lucy.

MRS. RANDALL

What do you mean?

RHODA
(*With some enjoyment*)
I mean, he's tried to pinch *me,* too.

MRS. RANDALL
I don't believe it! I don't believe a word of it! This is something you've made up—both of you. Do you mean he tried to be—familiar?

CALLA
That'll do as well as any other word.

RHODA
Yes, Aunt Lucy. That's exactly what I mean!

MRS. RANDALL
Well, all I can say is—if he has, which I still don't believe, and never will—it was your own fault. No gentleman is ever familiar with a lady unless she has cheapened herself with him. Perhaps he had reason to believe that it was—what you were accustomed to! (*The girls' mouths open*) I shall not forgive your telling me that, Calla. Or you, either, Rhoda! (*She goes out with dignity.*)

CALLA
Well, I guess that takes care of us! When did you start cheapening yourself?

167

RHODA

Last night, I imagine.

CALLA

Oh, yes, what was that all about? You and Neil?

RHODA

Calla, I've been into that twice already this morning. Do you mind?

CALLA

Not a bit. Well, I guess I'd better get dressed.

RHODA

Calla, why did you tell Jimmy last night that his mother didn't like you?

CALLA

I thought it was time he knew.

RHODA

Why?

CALLA

Because I mean to break that up.

RHODA

That's going to hurt Jimmy, if you do.

CALLA

He'll get over it.

RHODA

Are you in love with him?

CALLA

What's that got to do with it?

RHODA

Everything, I should think. You're not, are you? What are you marrying him for?

CALLA

If you want to know, that's what I've been asking myself these last weeks.

RHODA

Do you think you're going to be happy with him?

CALLA
(*With a shrug*)
It'll be all right—I guess.

RHODA

You're not sure?

CALLA

What are all these questions?

RHODA

Nothing. Only I just thought, last night—that it didn't look like a very good prospect to me.

CALLA

Do you think I'm a fool to go through with it?

RHODA

From your point of view? I don't know. I don't know what you expect from it.

CALLA

I'll tell you. I expect exactly what I'll get. Security. Enough money to live on. Not having to worry about the rent, or whether I get a job for the next three months or not. Not having handkerchiefs drying all over the mirrors, or going without lunch to get my gloves cleaned, or my shoes fixed.

RHODA

Yes, you'll get that.

CALLA

The trouble is that for the last three months, I've had it, and it bores the hell out of me. You see, he isn't really rich. That's the snag. I didn't realize it at first. It looked like riches to me. But it isn't. He's just—comfortably off. And that's not good enough. You're really rich. You know.

RHODA

Do you mean you want to get out of it?

CALLA

I mean, I'd like to, but I think I'd be a fool. In six

months' time, I'd be back exactly where I am. I'd thought of driving *him* to breaking it off. For what I could get out of it. But it wouldn't be enough. I wouldn't settle for less than twenty-five thousand. I could get that in court. But he couldn't pay it. Nor could his mother. I know that.

RHODA
(*Quietly*)

I could.

CALLA

What did you say?

RHODA

I said I could.

CALLA

What do you mean?

RHODA

I mean that if you'll take twenty-five thousand dollars to break off your engagement, I'll give it to you.

CALLA

What for?

RHODA

Because I think the whole thing is a horrible mistake. You don't want to marry Jimmy, and he doesn't want to marry you.

CALLA

Did he tell you so?

171

RHODA

I've got eyes of my own.

CALLA

But why should *you* fork over?

RHODA

Because I'm fond of him, and I don't want to see him unhappy.

CALLA

Are you in love with him?

RHODA

Don't be so silly!

CALLA

Well, I knew you were rich, but . . .

RHODA

Look, you said you'd take twenty-five thousand. If you will, I'll give you a check on my bank in London. I'll give it to you now. (*She goes for her pocketbook*) I've got my checkbook here. Will you take it?

CALLA

Wait a minute. I've got to think this over.

RHODA

All right, but in that case, I can think it over, too. You'd better take it while you can.

CALLA

I don't get this.

RHODA

Will you take it?

CALLA

(*Very slowly*)

Make it thirty . . .

RHODA

Thirty? That's—six thousand pounds. All right.

CALLA

You don't mean it.

RHODA

I'll write the check now. (*She goes to the desk*) I shall have to send a cable, but it'll be all right. I can promise you that. What's the date?

CALLA

December the fifteenth.

RHODA

(*Writing the check*)

By the way, there's one thing that I'd like to know. It's not important, but . . .

CALLA

What is it?

RHODA

All these stories about your having been so virtuous in the face of temptation—were they true?

CALLA

Yes, of course they were.

RHODA

Really? It won't make any difference to this—(*Indicating the check*) if they weren't, you know. As I say, it isn't important, but I'd like to know for my own satisfaction. I think I'm entitled to something out of this, too, aren't I?

CALLA

What do you want to know?

RHODA

Had you really always been—straight, till you met Jimmy?

CALLA

Yes. That is—at least . . .

RHODA

(*With quiet, silky satisfaction*)

That's all. That's all I wanted to know. I thought you hadn't—quite. (*She finishes the check, blots and tears it out and then rises and hands it over*) Here. (CALLA *takes it, staring at it, speechless*) Now, is it settled?

CALLA

What do I do now?

RHODA

You tell Jimmy that you've changed your mind, and that you want to break off the engagement. And you don't tell him about *that*. Naturally.

CALLA

No. Naturally.

RHODA

That's all.

CALLA

(*Folds the check, places it in her bosom, and speaks dazedly*)
Well—thanks.

RHODA

(*Ironically*)
Don't mention it.

CALLA

(*Coming slowly out of her trance*)
There's something back of all this.

RHODA

What do you mean?

CALLA

(*Slowly*)
You are in love with him. You must be. All this time. Why did I never think of it before?

RHODA

Don't be absurd!

CALLA

That's why I've never been able to make you out! That's why you've nursed him through all his affairs! It's true, isn't it?

RHODA

(*After a moment*)

All right, then. It's true. I've always been in love with him. I've known it never could come to anything, but— if he's unhappy with you, at least I can get him out of it. That's all.

CALLA

Don't try and pull the wool over my eyes! Well, I've heard of American girls going to England and buying husbands for themselves but . . .

RHODA

(*Appalled and aghast*)

What? Is that what you think? (*Reaching for the check, in an access of horror*) Give me that back!

CALLA

(*Retreating*)

You're just paying me off, to leave the coast clear for yourself! And what a hope you've got!

RHODA

(*Starting after her*)

You nasty little demi-rep!

CALLA

(*Dodging her round the couch*)

Me? And what do you think you are? Spooning in hansom-cabs with men!

RHODA

(*Chasing her; murderously*)

If I get my hands on you . . .

CALLA

(*Still dodging*)

So this is the famous temper that I've heard about!

RHODA

You'll do more than hear about it, in a minute! (*The chase continues. A table goes over.* RHODA *catches her.*)

RHODA

(*Shaking her*)

Now, then, you'll take back what you said!

CALLA

I won't! (*She pulls her hair.*)

RHODA

(*Grabbing at* CALLA's *hair*)

Let go! Let go! (*She bites her.* CALLA *screams and lets go of her hair. They go into a clinch, and wrestle. Another piece of furniture goes over, and they go with it, rolling*) *on the floor, struggling with each other. Banging* CALLA's *head on the floor*) Now then. Take it back! Take it back!

(*The door opens and* JIMMY *appears, his coat off, and shaving soap on his face.*)

JIMMY

Hey, what's going on? Rhoda! Calla! What are you doing? (*He rushes forward and starts to separate them.* RHODA *leaps up, staring at him for a moment, wide-eyed and stricken. He lays his hand on her arm*) Rhoda, what's the matter? Rhoda! (*She shakes him off. Again he touches her*) Rhoda! What is it?

RHODA
(*Flinging him off, violently*)

Oh, go to hell! (*She dashes out of the room, leaving him staring after her.* CALLA *is sitting up on the floor. In the doorway, as* RHODA *rushes out,* MRS. RANDALL *appears, also staring after her.*)

CURTAIN

ACT THREE

Scene II

Scene: *The same. Around three-thirty the same afternoon.* Michael *is discovered, reading a novel on the couch. Enter* Jimmy.

Jimmy

Hello. What are you reading?

Michael

It's a new book by H. G. Wells. I found it in Daph's room. I don't think much of it. It's called *Ann Veronica*.

Jimmy
(*Amused*)

Oh—well, don't let Mother catch you with that.

Michael
(*With astonishment*)

Why, do you mean it's—hot stuff?

Jimmy

Well, it's considered . . . advanced.

MICHAEL

(*Flipping the pages*)

Oh, I can't have come to the bad part, then. I wasn't going to finish it.

JIMMY

But now you will, eh? Well, hide it, or else put brown paper round it, with *The Five Little Peppers* on the outside. (*He looks around*) Where is everyone?

MICHAEL

Mother's lying down with a headache. Daph's in her room, and Rhoda's out some place. Jimmy, what's happened?

JIMMY

Happened?

MICHAEL

Well, Mother's awfully upset about something. You know she was going to take us out to lunch. Well, she said she wasn't well enough, and sent Daph and me out alone. We went to Huyler's. I had three Knickerbocker Glories. Daph's upset over something, too. It's to do with Rhoda, isn't it?

JIMMY

What makes you think that?

MICHAEL

Well, Mother said something to Daph. She said Rhoda had compromised herself. Is that true?

JIMMY

Well, Mother thinks it is.

MICHAEL

What does that mean, exactly?

JIMMY

Oh, it means that—well, that her reputation's damaged. It's a lot of nonsense.

MICHAEL

It's an awful thing for a girl, isn't it—to be compromised?

JIMMY

It's supposed to be.

MICHAEL

It's worse than being—fast?

JIMMY

I should say it was a natural consequence.

MICHAEL

You don't mean that they . . . ?

JIMMY

What?

MICHAEL

Well, that Neil—seduced her?

JIMMY
(*Jumping*)

Good God Almighty, no! Whatever put that into your head?

MICHAEL

I just thought . . .

JIMMY

You really are a little idiot. What opportunity did he have to seduce her, anyway?

MICHAEL

I thought perhaps they went to a hotel.

JIMMY

Really, what do you think people are?

MICHAEL

Well, I know Neil does have girls . . .

JIMMY

How do you know?

MICHAEL

You've told me.

JIMMY
(*Momentarily deflated*)

Oh! (*Then, rallying*) I tell you a damn sight too much, if that's the kind of thing it makes you think up!

And Rhoda, of all people! One of the things you've got to learn as you grow up, my boy, is the difference between a good woman and a bad one, or you'll get yourself into the most awful messes.

MICHAEL

How does one tell?

JIMMY

One doesn't tell. One knows.

MICHAEL

How?

JIMMY

I don't know how. One does.

MICHAEL

What was all the racket down here this morning? I'd just gotten up, and it sounded as though there was a fight going on. It was Rhoda and Calla, wasn't it? What was that about?

JIMMY

Look, Michael, if I give you fifty cents, will you go and get yourself three more Knickerbocker Glories, and stop asking questions?

MICHAEL

I only wanted to know.

183

JIMMY

Well, I'm afraid you've come to the wrong quarter. I don't know any more than you do. And if I did, I wouldn't tell you.

MICHAEL

Didn't you ask Calla what it was about?

JIMMY

I did. And she wouldn't tell me. So put that in your little pipe and smoke it. (*He opens the door, and then speaks very casually*) By the way, you may be interested to know that Calla and I aren't engaged any more.

MICHAEL

What?

JIMMY

That's all. (*He goes out.* MICHAEL, *alone, sits open-mouthed for a moment. Then he rises, goes after him to the door, calling:* "JIMMY! JIMMY!" DAPHNE *comes in, and they almost collide.*)

DAPHNE

What's eating you?

MICHAEL

Daph, Jimmy says that he and Calla aren't engaged any more.

DAPHNE

No? Why, what's happened?

MICHAEL

I don't know. He didn't say. I was just going up to ask him.

DAPHNE

When did this happen?

MICHAEL

I don't know. Today, I suppose. He took her out to lunch, didn't he? They were engaged all right last night.

DAPHNE

She must have broken it off at lunch, then.

MICHAEL

Or else *he* did.

DAPHNE

No, it's always the girl who breaks off the engagement.

MICHAEL

Is it? Oh! Say, you never told me this was an immoral book.

DAPHNE

I only finished it this morning.

MICHAEL

What happens? Does she have a baby?

DAPHNE

No. At least not until after they're married. But she

goes away with a married man that she's in love with. She tells him she's in love with him. He says, "What is it you want?" and she says, "You," and then they go away.

(*Enter* NEIL.)

NEIL

Hello, there.

DAPHNE
(*With a jump*)

Oh, hello.

NEIL

They said Jimmy was up here.

MICHAEL

He's in his room.

NEIL

Actually, it was Miss Meldrum I came to see.

DAPHNE

She's out.

NEIL

I know. I thought I'd wait for her.

MICHAEL

I'm going up to Jimmy. I'll tell him you're here.

NEIL

Don't bother him. Daphne will keep me company, I'm sure.

MICHAEL

It's all right. (*He goes out.*)

NEIL

How are you today? Have you gotten over the party?

DAPHNE
(*Constrainedly*)

Yes, thanks.

NEIL

Will Rhoda be long, do you know?

DAPHNE

I don't know. I haven't seen her today.

NEIL

I telephoned her at lunchtime. I didn't imagine she'd be up before. But she was out.

DAPHNE

Yes. (*Then, with sudden resolution and directness*) Are you in love with her?

NEIL
(*With an astonished laugh*)

Good Lord, whatever makes you think that?

DAPHNE
(*With an odd tenseness*)

I want to know.

NEIL

(*Lightly*)

Why, I hardly know her. I only met her yesterday.

DAPHNE

Yes, I know. But—you still could be.

NEIL

I think she's very charming.

DAPHNE

You haven't answered my question.

NEIL

Daphne, that's ridiculous.

DAPHNE

You and she went off together somewhere last night.

NEIL

We went for a drive round the Park. But you don't think—because of that . . .

DAPHNE

You're not in love with her? You don't want to marry her?

NEIL

Why, I never thought of such a thing!

DAPHNE

(*Walks away from him; then after a moment, with her back to him, she speaks in a tight, determined little voice*)

I'm in love with *you*.

NEIL

What? Daphne!

DAPHNE

(*As before*)

I am.

NEIL

Daphne, you can't be!

DAPHNE

Yes, I can. I have been—for a long time.

NEIL

But you don't know what you're saying.

DAPHNE

Yes, I do. (*She turns to him*) I'm in love with you. That's why I asked you about Rhoda. If you'd said yes, I wouldn't have told you. But if you're not in love with her . . .

NEIL

I'm not in love with anyone.

189

DAPHNE

That's what I thought. That's why I told you.

NEIL

(*Very kindly*)

Yes, but, Daphne—it's very, very sweet of you, but it's crazy.

DAPHNE

(*Tightly*)

Is it?

NEIL

You're just a kid . . .

DAPHNE

I'm not—any more.

NEIL

Compared to me, you are.

DAPHNE

You mean—you couldn't care for me?

NEIL

I'm very fond of you, but . . .

DAPHNE

But that's all—all you could ever be?

NEIL

Daphne, what is it you want?

DAPHNE
(*White with strain*)
I want *you.* (*There is a moment of absolute silence;
then everything drains from her*) Yes, it does sound
silly, like that. I'll go. (*She starts for the door.*)

NEIL
(*Catching her and detaining her*)
Daphne, listen. I'm very, very touched at your feeling
like this, but—it's all wrong.

DAPHNE

I know. Please let me go.

NEIL

Not for a minute.

DAPHNE

Please. Please. I've been a fool. Don't make me stay
here.

NEIL

But, Daphne . . . (RHODA *comes in.* NEIL *releases*
DAPHNE, *who flies from the room.* RHODA *looks after
her with surprise*) Good afternoon.

RHODA

Good afternoon. What's the matter with Daphne?

191

NEIL

I think she's upset about something.

RHODA

(*Still looking after her, worriedly*)

I haven't seen her since last night. Did she say anything?

NEIL

What about?

RHODA

About us, or—our—escapade.

NEIL

She—mentioned it.

RHODA

I should have thought of that. (*She takes off her furs, distressedly.*)

NEIL

Well, don't let's talk about her. How are you today?

RHODA

I'm all right. Thank you for your flowers. They gave them to me downstairs. And thank you for your help last night. For staying on.

NEIL

You're welcome. Did you have trouble this morning?

192

RHODA

A little.

NEIL

But you managed. (*He goes to her*) What are you looking so worried about? (*He puts his arms around her*) Rhoda! Rhoda! (*He tries to kiss her.*)

RHODA
(*Astonished*)
What on earth are you doing?

NEIL

I'm trying to kiss you.

RHODA

Well, please don't. (*She releases herself.*)

NEIL

Why not?

RHODA

Because I don't like it.

NEIL

You let me last night.

RHODA

Last night was last night. This is this afternoon.

193

NEIL

Do I have to wait till six o'clock—like the first drink?

RHODA

(*Facing him*)

Mr. Harding . . .

NEIL

Oh, not Mr. Harding . . .

RHODA

(*Firmly*)

Mr. Harding, I've got to be very frank with you.

NEIL

Shoot.

RHODA

I don't know what you're thinking, or—expecting, but this can't go any further.

NEIL

Why not?

RHODA

Because I don't want it to.

NEIL

Are you regretting last night?

RHODA

No. Not at all. But it's over.

NEIL

You mean you don't want to see me again?

RHODA

I think it would be better not. In any case, I shan't be here very long. I'm going back to England.

NEIL

When?

RHODA

Next week.

NEIL

But you've only just come. This hasn't anything to do with—last night, has it?

RHODA

Not in the sense you mean. Not at all, really.

NEIL

Why, then?

RHODA
(*Uncomfortably*)

Well, largely on account of something that happened this morning, but—I'd rather not go into that.

NEIL

Will you let me take you out before you go?

RHODA

I don't think so. Thank you.

NEIL

I wish you'd tell me what's the matter.

RHODA

There's nothing the matter. At least, not to do with you. I'm very grateful to you. Really I am.

NEIL

For what, for God's sake?

RHODA

For last night. You were very flattering. You said very charming things, and I wanted to hear them. You gave me an adventure that I shall always remember. Driving round Central Park in the snow with you, and being made love to—very charmingly. You do make love charmingly.

NEIL

Are you kidding me?

RHODA

Indeed, no. I'm saying thank you.

NEIL

Then why won't you see me again?

RHODA

Because one glass of champagne is enough.

NEIL

It's not, for me.

RHODA

Well, there it is.

NEIL

Is that all it was—a glass of champagne?

RHODA

What could be nicer? Does that hurt your feelings?

NEIL

(*With slight amusement*)

Not my—feelings.

RHODA

Your vanity?

NEIL

You *are* making fun of me.

RHODA

Well, perhaps a very little. Do you mind?

NEIL

(*With a touch of wry humor*)

I'm not used to it . . .

RHODA

From girls? I'm sorry, but—don't grudge me that little triumph over the others.
(*Enter* JIMMY.)

JIMMY

Michael just told me you were here.

RHODA

I must go upstairs. (*To* NEIL) I'll say good-bye.

NEIL

Good-bye.

RHODA

And thank you again so much—(*With the merest hint of a pause*)—for the flowers. (*She goes.*)

JIMMY

Surely this is very old-world of you—calling the day after a dance?

NEIL

(*Bursting out*)
I shall never understand English women!

JIMMY

Oh, what's the trouble?

NEIL

Your cousin. What is she?

JIMMY

Well, in Mother's phrase, she's a very nice girl—there's nothing wrong with her. (*With a thought*) Although I think Mother's revised that opinion since last night. (*With another*) *And* this morning. I'm even beginning to revise it a bit, myself. What was the idea of you and her going off last night, by the way?

NEIL

An impulse.

JIMMY

Damn fool one.

NEIL

Have you never had an impulse to whirl a girl away from a ballroom?

JIMMY

Sure. Not Rhoda, though.

NEIL

You think of her the way I do about my sister, don't you?

JIMMY

Yes, I think I do—from that point of view.

NEIL

Well, that's where you're wrong. Alice would never behave the way she did last night.

199

JIMMY
(*Astonished*)

You mean . . . ?

NEIL

I mean.

JIMMY
(*Incredulous*)

Rhoda?

NEIL

Rhoda.

JIMMY

You mean you made love to her? (NEIL *nods*) And she let you? (NEIL *nods again*) What do you mean—"making love?"

NEIL

I mean "making love." Romantic love, in a hansom. You've done it yourself. You know. And then this afternoon when I expect some kind of follow-up, she quietly tells me that "That's all there is, there isn't any more." Not that it was all a mistake, and should never have happened, and that she can't think what she was doing . . .

JIMMY
(*Exploding somewhat*)

Well, *I* can't think what she was doing. Or you, either.

NEIL
(*Astonished*)

Hey!

JIMMY
(*Rather pompously*)

No, damn it, I mean it. You don't do that sort of thing with decent girls in decent houses. And decent girls don't let you.

NEIL

Jimmy, what's happened to your sense of humor?

JIMMY

What's my sense of humor got to do with it?

NEIL

Everything. You've never gone self-righteous like this before.

JIMMY

You've never pulled a trick like this before.

NEIL

Jimmy, she's not a kid of eighteen. She knows how many beans make five.

JIMMY
(*As before*)

And that's no way to talk about her, either.

NEIL

Oh! Sorry!

JIMMY

(*Coming out of it a little*)

No, but honestly, can't you see the difference between a girl like Rhoda, and—the kind of girl you can do that sort of thing with?

NEIL

Jimmy, you won't hit me if I repeat that the whole point is that she turns out to *be* the kind of girl you can do that sort of thing with?

JIMMY

You don't mean . . . ?

NEIL

I wouldn't know. If I'd had an apartment in New York that we could have gone to, instead of driving round Central Park, I might be able to answer you.

JIMMY

Rhoda would never go to a man's apartment.

NEIL

Not this afternoon. But last night . . . Well, as I say, I don't know. And I guess I never shall. Oh, well . . .

JIMMY

Well, I'm certainly seeing a lot of new sides to her, all of a sudden.

NEIL
(*Lightly*)
Feel like making love to her yourself now?

JIMMY
Don't be a fool!

NEIL
Well, there are folks who don't find anyone attractive till someone else tells them that they are.

JIMMY
(*Huffily*)
I know who attracts me, and who doesn't, thank you.

NEIL
Like the guys who don't find a woman attractive till she's got a bad reputation.

JIMMY
(*A trifle sourly*)
I thought that was *you*.

NEIL
(*Sunnily*)
I think it's all of us. You know, it was really Michael's idea of Rhoda that first interested me in her.

JIMMY
(*Contemptuously*)
What does Michael know about her?

NEIL
I think Michael's at the age where he believes that any
girl's potentially a bad girl. Maybe he's not so far wrong.

JIMMY
(*Holding out to the last*)
Not Rhoda!

NEIL
Well . . . You know she's going back to England?

JIMMY
When?

NEIL
She said next week.

JIMMY
No, no. She's going to Indianapolis. At least, that's
the idea.

NEIL
She said England.

JIMMY
She meant Indianapolis.

NEIL
They sound so alike. Well, now I'll get along.

JIMMY

Are you going back to Boston?

NEIL

Might as well. There's nothing to stay here for.

JIMMY

Call me next time you're in town.

NEIL

Sure. Give my love to Calla, by the way.

JIMMY

Oh . . . (*He is about to tell* NEIL *the news, then thinks better of it*) Sure.

NEIL

What were you going to say?

JIMMY

Nothing—now. It'll keep.

NEIL

Everything all right there?

JIMMY

Sure.

(*Enter* RHODA. *She has changed into an afternoon frock.*)

205

NEIL

Well, good-bye, then.

RHODA

I'm not driving you away, am I?

NEIL

No. I have to go. Good-bye again.

RHODA

Good-bye.
(NEIL *goes.* RHODA *sits and takes up her work.*
JIMMY *stares at her, as though seeing her suddenly
anew and for the first time.*)

JIMMY
(*After a silence*)

Rhoda . . .

RHODA

Jimmy, I want to apologize for this morning.

JIMMY

Oh, that's all right. What was that all about?

RHODA

Didn't Calla tell you?

JIMMY

She said you'd had a row. She said you'd make it up

206

afterwards, upstairs. She wouldn't tell me what it was about.

RHODA

Well, if you don't mind, I'd rather not, either. But I'm sorry.

JIMMY

Rhoda, I've something to tell you. You know what we were talking about this morning—about Calla . . . ?

RHODA

Yes?

JIMMY

Well, apparently she's realized it, too. That it wouldn't work, I mean. She said a lot of things to me today at lunch. And—she's broken it off.

RHODA
(*Quietly*)

I see.

JIMMY

You don't sound surprised.

RHODA

Well, I don't think I am—really. It was quite obvious, Jimmy, that it wasn't any use, and Calla's a sensible girl. What did she say?

JIMMY

Just that she knew it wasn't any good. That we'd never

get along together, and that she wanted to call it off. I asked her what she was going to do—how she was going to live . . .

RHODA

(*Holding her breath*)

And she said?

JIMMY

She said she'd be all right. She'll go back to the stage. I wanted to make some sort of—settlement or something, but she wouldn't take it.

RHODA

I like her for that.

JIMMY

Oh, Calla's all right in lots of ways. It's just that—as a wife, she wouldn't do. For me, anyway. It was just the wrapping I liked. It's the most extraordinary feeling to be free again. I can't believe it. It's such luck!

RHODA

(*Subduedly*)

I'm glad you're glad.

JIMMY

Free to go back and—start again. (*Then with a thought*) Rhoda, what's this about your going back to England?

RHODA

Oh, did Mr. Harding tell you?

208

JIMMY

You mean it's true? (*She nods*) But you've only just come.

RHODA

I know, but . . .

JIMMY

What?

RHODA

Well, after the way I've behaved . . .

JIMMY

You mean last night?

RHODA

And this morning.

JIMMY

I wish you'd tell me what this morning was about.

RHODA

That's not important. But I lost my temper—very badly. Calla was very nice about it afterwards. . .

JIMMY

Oh, that kind of thing doesn't mean anything to Calla.

RHODA

Well, it does to me. And I feel horrible about it. Dirty and ashamed.

JIMMY

Is that why you want to go home?

RHODA

That on top of everything else. It's all turned out all wrong. My whole visit here.

JIMMY

Has this anything to do with Neil?

RHODA

No. It hasn't anything to do with anyone—except myself. I'm disgusted with myself from every point of view. I'm nothing like the kind of person that I thought I was, and I don't like what I turn out to be—*at all*. I'm not even a lady!

JIMMY
(*Impatiently*)

Oh, what rubbish!

RHODA

No, it's true. I can't stay here. I booked my passage this afternoon—sailing next week on the *Baltic*. I'll get around to all the necessary lies and arrangements with Aunt Lucy later. I shall probably have a bad cold between now and leaving.

JIMMY

Mother's not sending you home?

RHODA

No, but she won't stop me going.

JIMMY

But it's ridiculous. I don't want you to go. God knows when we'll meet again. And just now when I'm suddenly seeing you quite differently for the first time . . . (*She looks up*) You know it's crazy the way we've always been brought up as—brother and sister, almost. . . . It's stopped our ever seeing each other as anything else. At least, it's stopped me—till now.

RHODA

Why now?

JIMMY

I don't know. I guess because—the wrapping's changed.

RHODA
(*Bewildered*)

What?

JIMMY

I've always taken you so completely for granted. But now, if you wouldn't go . . .

RHODA

What do you mean—"If I wouldn't go?"

JIMMY

Well, I'd kinda like to start off on a different foot, if

that wouldn't seem too silly to you. Oh, I know you've never thought of me that way. I wouldn't know how to make myself romantic to you, but—that's what you've become to me. (*Looking at her and speaking with a kind of surprised puzzlement*) I've always known you had all the other things, but I've never realized before that you're really very attractive, too. You're the kind of girl I want to marry.

RHODA
(*Suddenly, after one perfect moment*)
Jimmy, who put you up to this?

JIMMY
No one. I just think I've been completely blind, that's all.

RHODA
No one's said anything?

JIMMY
Do you mean Mother? Oh, she's often hinted . . . I know she'd like us to get married.

RHODA
Not any more.

JIMMY
Oh, she'd get over that, if we did. (*Solemnly*) I'll help you live the scandal down.

(RHODA *goes into a mild case of hysterics.*)

212

RHODA
(*Half-laughing, half-crying*)
Oh, Jimmy.

JIMMY
(*Alarmed*)
What's the matter?

RHODA
(*As before*)
You've such a passion for tarnished women!

JIMMY
That's a hell of a thing to say—now. (*He turns away, a little hurt and sulky.*)

RHODA
(*Coaxingly*)
Jimmy, I don't mind. It's rather nice to be . . . tinsel, for once. (*He starts back toward her, but is stopped by the entrance of* NORA, *with the lace teacloth. She goes over for the table, places it where it was in Act One, and lays the cloth. Feigning heartiness*) Oh, here's tea. Good! (*She resumes her tapestry.*)

JIMMY
(*In Cockney tones, referring to the tapestry*)
'Ow's Grandma Meldrum coming on?

RHODA

(*Also Cockney*)

Well, I was thinking. 'Er eyesight ain't what it used to be. If I was to buy 'er a piece, I don't think she'd know no different. And (*In her own voice*) I could give this up—if you really hate it.

NORA

Will Miss Longstreth be here for tea, Mr. Jimmy?

JIMMY

Oh—er—no, Nora. No, she won't.

NORA

It'll be just the five cups, then. (*She goes out for the tray.*)

JIMMY

I do wish I knew what your row with Calla was about.

RHODA

That, Jimmy, is something that I'll never tell you.

JIMMY

Not even when we're married?

RHODA

(*Smiling at him*)

Not even when we're married!

(NORA *returns with the tea tray.*)

CURTAIN